Randa Abdel-Fattal
the Department of … at Macquarie University,
where she is researching the generational impact of the war on terror on Muslim and non-Muslim youth born into a post 9/11 world. She is a prominent anti-racism and Palestine advocate and a multi-award-winning author of eleven young adult and children's books published in over sixteen countries. Randa is currently working on the film adaptation of her novel *Does My Head Look Big in This?* and is keen to use her intervention into popular culture to reshape dominant narratives around race.

Sara Saleh is a poet and activist. A campaigner for refugee rights and racial justice, she has spent the past decade working with Amnesty International and CARE International in Australia and the Middle East. She is currently completing her Juris Doctor, developing her debut novel and is a proud Bankstown Poetry Slam 'Slambassador'.

ARAB

STORIES ON

AUSTRALIAN

RACE AND IDENTITY

OTHER

EDITED BY
RANDA ABDEL-FATTAH
AND SARA SALEH

PICADOR
Pan Macmillan Australia

First published 2019 in Picador by Pan Macmillan Australia Pty Ltd
1 Market Street, Sydney, New South Wales, Australia, 2000

Printed by IVE

NATIONAL LIBRARY OF AUSTRALIA
A catalogue record for this book is available from the National Library of Australia

Typeset in 12.2/17pt Garamond by Post Pre-press Group, Brisbane
Printed by McPherson's Printing Group
'Seventy-One Years of Words' by Randa Abdel-Fattah was originally published on *ABC Religion & Ethics* on 10 May 2018. It is reprinted here with permission.
'Of "Middle-Eastern Appearance"' was originally published on *Right Now* (rightnow.org.au) in May 2015. It is reprinted here with permission.

Poetry quoted on page 244 from *Unfortunately, It Was Paradise* © Mahmoud Darwish, reprinted by permission of University of California Press Books.

Aboriginal and Torres Strait Islander people should be aware that this book may contain names of people now deceased. Specifically, Introduction, 'You Don't Look Lebanese' and 'Holding the Line'.

To the families of Diaspora,
may we always have stories to tell.

Contents

Introduction

Anthologies can function like time capsules. An excavation of stories, testimonies and memories, they offer us a sense of people's everyday lives at a particular juncture in time, an understanding of who we were – and who we are. While many of the writers and poets in this collection weave in and between different stages of their lives, there is a distinct time – place feeling that lingers over this anthology. A feeling that most of the voices who are speaking to us belong to a distinct generational category. Not in the sense of an age cohort, but in the sense that this is a generation of lives distinctly shaped and shadowed by a post 9/11 world.

The stories brought together here are dynamic and self-determined, but most are also inescapably haunted by the spectre of a nation, indeed a world, in which the word 'Arab' is more accusation than identity. Even those stories which began in the 1970s and 80s play out here with different endings to those likely imagined by writers prior to 9/11. From defining oneself as not-ethnic-gangster, not-drug-dealer, not-rapist; to 'jaywalking Arab' or playing Aladdin in the school playground. To the ache and pain of being named, of being denied one's name, of changing one's name. To being Lebanese . . . but, Muslim . . . but, hijabi . . . but. To speak of 'coming out Palestinian', or painting flowers as a political, feminist act. To aerobics and hair removal or one's work supervisor politely questioning if you plan to join ISIS. All of these stories are located in the particular context of a world at war on terror, at war *with* and *on* 'the Middle East'.

And yet . . . can the metaphor of a time capsule really capture what it is to be Arab-Australian-Other? For can Western colonialism be contained? Will there ever be a time when the scars, agonies, ghosts and intergenerational trauma are capable of being sealed into a historical moment?

Palestine, Iraq, Syria, Yemen . . . colonialism, imperialism, the war on terror, the Arab revolutions and their quashing, offshore detention centres (torture chambers): all of this *is* – not was. It *is* now, as the contributors created their pieces, as we write this introduction, as you read this book. A first-year university student in Sydney recites her own lest we forget: the names of her family members lost at sea. We reflect on what it means to be hyphenated, even in death. Another writes on the death of his father who never had a chance to return to his occupied homeland, Palestine. It is clear that to write about what it means to be Arab-Australian-Other is like trying to rake leaves on a windy day. Just as soon as you capture some peace within yourself, you are at risk of being scattered by the winds of imperialism and war.

*

Oh but Arabs are a resilient bunch. And the women. The women! 'Revolting women.' Agitators, rebels – rocking, shaking, capsizing the 'patriarchal boat'. Women fighting Islamophobia and anti-Arab racism on the outside, and women fighting anti-blackness, colourism and racism on the inside, within the Arab community. Women who stand up to expectations about who they should and should not marry, and women who negotiate bumping into unwanted male suitors at the Arab-Aussie 'unifying' equivalent of the local pub – a Free Palestine Protest.

The Arab-Australian-Others in this book spend a lot of their lives being subversive: subverting norms around gender, sexuality, race and religion. And yet the joy, humour and wisdom with which they share their battles illustrates time and again that they refuse to be defined or even to define themselves.

Edward Said tells us: 'No-one today is purely one thing. Labels like Indian, or woman, or Muslim, or American are not more than starting-points, which if followed into actual experience for only a moment are quickly left behind . . . Yet just as human beings make their own history, they also make their cultures and ethnic identities'. Within the pages of this book are human beings who are clearly more than 'purely one thing' – there is a before, and an after, an ongoing. Perhaps the most liberation a human being can hope for is the freedom of fluidity.

Although we hail from over twenty-two different countries, many exist in the spaces between borders, and represent a wide variety of cultural backgrounds and experiences. Racism's cartography of Others – from 'integration' to 'assimilation', dismissal to erasure – the identity of the 'Arab' is not without its stereotypes, its scapegoating, its moulding into whatever 'other' is needed in the narrative of successful, multicultural Australia where the dispositions and configurations of (cultural) power are always shifting. Here, representation is a 'crucial location of struggle'.

Through these stories we are redefining and reclaiming this. It is clear the contributors have much to say. This anthology is a conversation, and we finally get to speak to ourselves.

As a result of a national callout for contributions, we received eighty submissions from individuals who identify as Arab and we thank all of them for trusting us with their stories. We did not place any limitations on the submissions beyond asking for memoirs, personal essays, critical pieces and poetry. Writers from all walks of life offer their own narratives and highlight their continuing attempts at carving a sense of self in a space whose parameters are already seemingly set for them, whether by their own community or by the outside/mainstream.

The collection is guided by our contributors, whose multitude of experiences are impossible to locate on a map, yet rooted into consciousness. Their stories are told with the catharsis of ritual, with the wisdom and hope of a prayer, with the survival, strength and vulnerability of an ongoing journey.

*

With this anthology we wanted to push beyond the rhetoric of a celebratory multiculturalism that co-opts and cannibalises 'diversity' and denies Indigenous sovereignty. The racism, discrimination and exclusion these writers describe was tested and practised (*is* practised) on Aboriginal bodies first. In curating these stories, we chose voices that would shake up conventional narratives about what it means to belong as a minority. From a café in 'dystopian Egypt' where an Australian-Egyptian deliberates on the 'coffins of sorrow' burying Gika, Asmaa and Mina in Egypt, and Doomadgee, TJ Hickey, Ms Dhu in Australia; to the centering of 'women whose backs have been broken by our presence here' and the acknowledgment of 'the suffering we have collectively caused to the First Peoples of the Land', we are, as one contributor writes, 'migrant settlers'. This is an anthology that reflects on our privileges and debts as Arab-Australians. When reading the stories gathered here, we hope readers are provoked to think about this nation's histories that have enabled and disabled these writers from speaking and living on their own terms today. And so, we start with Arab-Australian-Other, but we end by humbly acknowledging that this anthology was conceived, written, edited and published on unceded land.

Randa Abdel-Fattah and *Sara Saleh*

__Ruby Hamad__ is a journalist, author and PhD student in media studies at UNSW. A former Fairfax columnist, her work also appears in Meanjin, The Saturday Paper, SBS, Crikey *and* The Guardian. *She is a columnist for* The New Arab *and her first book* White Tears/Brown Scars *was published by MUP in September 2019.*

The Third Time I Broke My Father's Heart

The first time I pretended I wasn't an Arab was sort of a mistake. Sort of. At all of twenty years of age I – or hang on, was it twenty-one? It was definitely before I turned twenty-two because by then I was gone, absconding from Australia shortly after graduating uni the first time with a one-way ticket in my hand and $2000 on my Keycard that shrank to $1000 without spending a cent because of all the planes I could have taken I took the one that landed at LAX. I would be away for almost four years. But that was yet to come. Right now, I am on a brand spanking new Tangara that is pulling into Martin Place. I see them whispering, trying to figure me out, but I pretend not to notice. My big yellow Walkman and headphones that fit like small earmuffs are my buffer against the world.

Finally, the woman comes over to where I grip the pole near the door. She says they are lost. They need directions. Please can I help them? I don't know where they want to get to – I can't understand everything she is trying to tell me. They don't speak English. My eyes widen and her husband – I assume – shakes his head. 'I told you she's not,' he admonishes. 'She is,' she shoots back, not missing a beat. 'Can you tell us where it is? How do we get there? We are lost.'

I'm stuck. It's been around two years since that morning I left for uni and didn't go back home again. I haven't spoken a word of Arabic in all that time. I haven't felt like an Arab in all that time. I wonder if she would understand how quickly your mother tongue can start to sound like that of a stranger. So I just shake my head again, making what I hope is a confused but friendly face.

'Sorry no. I'm not Arab.'

She frowns. He grabs her arm.

'I told you. Leave her.'

By now the train has stopped and commuters are pouring in and out. She looks into me. She knows. Why am I pretending? Why won't I help? He pulls her onto the platform. 'She is Arab. I'm telling you she is.' He gives a sheepish smile as the doors close and the train pulls away leaving a small audience to watch me make a show of turning over the Simple Minds Greatest Hits cassette tape.

There is a white girl opposite me, maybe my age maybe a bit older, and she smiles sympathetically as if we share a secret. The train picks up speed, eager as I am to leave the platform behind. 'Don't worry,' she consoles me assuredly so the whole vestibule can hear, '*I* don't think you look Arabic.'

Alive and Kicking. Jim Kerr's baritone is warbled from years of constant replay but it fills my ears like a warm blanket. The white girl beams at me. I stare out the window as we roar into the tunnel.

The first time they called me a terrorist it surprised them almost as much as it did me. It was the late 80s and more than a decade before Osama bin Laden would become a household name. My family is Alawite Muslim but back then this meant a lot less than the fact we are Lebanese. The Lebanese civil war was winding down, while the Israeli occupation of Palestine was ratcheting up. When my Macedonian classmate blurted out, 'Leh, you terrorist!' he had the grace to look stunned at his own slur. He was trying it out for size, I could tell even then. Seeing how the word fit, how it rolled off his tongue, how it affected me; would he keep this weapon on file to use again, or drop it as quickly as he'd reached for it?

It's not as bad as it sounds. During the 80s and 90s we were all 'wogs' even us Lebos. In my youth it was not my Muslimness that was contentious but my Arabness: the guttural language that grated on the delicate Anglo ear, the flat bread wrapped around pungent spreads and cheeses that was a poor substitute for the schoolyard requisite white slice and Kraft singles, and of course there was that name I so wished was not mine. But similar concerns were shared by my Vietnamese, Greek and Yugoslav friends – who could also be foes – too. We were always teasing each other. Greeks against Macedonians. Macedonians against Lebos. Lebos against Vietnamese. Some of us were picked on more than others, but that's just how it goes in the mean streets of high school, isn't it? We all got over it. Didn't we?

We both knew he wasn't calling me a terrorist because my family is Muslim but because we are Arab, that he was associating me not with Islam but with the Lebanese militias battling yet another incursion from their southern neighbour, and with the Palestinians that were letting Yasser Arafat's figurative olive branch fall from their hands as by now they needed both to grip the gun they thought was their last hope for freedom. And so they kidnapped Olympic athletes and hijacked aeroplanes and blew up buses in Jerusalem on the wild presumption that this would have to make the world stop and take note of their existence that was being systematically erased. It did, but not with the outcome they intended.

That boy never called me a terrorist again. The slur didn't quite fit then. I wonder if he would still think so today.

The first time I changed my name to Ruby I tried to spell it with an i. It was an impulsive decision, like so many of mine have been. That morning's art period was spent drawing on big rectangular sheets of white paper when I turned my middling creation over and scrawled *Rubi*, stylising the final letter with a circle rather than the standard dot plus adding an underline for emphasis. It was only one letter so I didn't expect my friends would make a big deal about it.

'Rubi!' one of them squealed. 'With an i!' Pretty soon all three were in hysterics. The worst thing to do now would be to react so I shrugged and wordlessly reached for the black marker to change the offending i back to the usual a. I never mentioned it again. Thankfully, neither did they.

The second time I changed my name to Ruby it kind of just happened. Kind of. Three years of university and working in cafes and Italian restaurants and meeting Anglo after Anglo who seemed to find my name too different or too difficult – all two syllables of it – and no sooner had the words 'I'm Ruba' left my lips than they were modifying it to something more familiar, something more like them. 'Ruby!' they'd greet me with delight sooner or later, not thinking to ask whether it was okay. After a while it just seemed to make sense to get there sooner, so I made it official and filled out the deed poll at the registry of births, deaths and marriages. This time I didn't spell it with an i.

The first time I remembered I was different was around the time I finished film school. I'd been to the other side of the world and back again and in those four years had decided my economics and social sciences degree was useless to me because I was going to be the next Jane Campion. That I was the only non-white student in my class of thirteen at the Victorian College of the Arts was not something I thought about much at the time, being more proud of seemingly overcoming my poor, Sydney inner-west roots to make it into the best film school in the country. Okay, second best, but we kidded ourselves otherwise.

For her twenty-fifth birthday a classmate threw a fancy dress party, which I usually avoid on principle; the principle being I can't stand them. This time though I had the perfect costume. The theme was Come as a Famous Work of Art and it was late summer in early 2007, just a couple of years after the Scarlett Johansson flick based on that old Dutch painting had decorated cinema screens. *Too easy*, I thought rather foolishly when I saw the cheap pair of imitation pearl drop-down earrings in the small chemist on the city end of Brunswick Street that isn't there anymore. Throw on an off-white long-sleeved collared shirt (you tend to have lots of these when you spend years of your life waiting tables) and the brilliant blue handmade shawl your friend Lynette had brought back for you from her month in India, and *voila*, there you are: the Girl With a Pearl Earring.

Except I'm no Scarlett Johansson. No-one had the faintest clue what I was meant to be. After four or five mystified appraisals and wrong guesses, it finally sunk in when the birthday girl, who although younger than me, smiled at me in that gentle way you do with a child who sincerely believes the surprise breakfast in bed of peanut butter and tomato sauce sandwiches they made for you is a gourmet feast.

In the bathroom I gazed at my reflection through their white eyes. Olive skin deeply bronzed by a long hot summer of laps in Fitzroy Pool. Big almost frog-like brown eyes. Oversized blue scarf that suddenly looked like a turban.

Dangling earring that signalled not a dainty maiden but an offensive Hollywood gypsy. I wasn't Girl With a Pearl Earring, I was Generic Wog Fortune Teller. I unwrapped the scarf and removed the earring. In my hip pocket it sat alongside its other half that I'd brought with me in case the first one fell out and ruined my costume. In the kitchen I poured myself the last of the white wine I'd brought with me. In the living room new artworks arranged themselves grandly on the vintage chaise longue.

'And what are you meant to be?'

'Nothing. Just myself.'

The first time I broke my father's heart was in year 9. For the first time ever we students were trusted to make decisions about our education and every kid in the year was to choose an elective subject. I elected to study Italian, a language that attracted me probably based on nothing other than it seemed less pretentious than French and more sophisticated than Spanish.

Also, it wasn't Arabic.

My father was beside himself. 'How could you choose another language? Are you not an Arab? Is Italian better than Arabic?' *Yes*, I wanted to retort but only muttered something about already doing Arabic at Saturday school. He couldn't understand. To him it was personal. I was rejecting my ancestry. I was rejecting my language. I was rejecting him. I couldn't tell him he was right. At least partly. As very young people often do, I picked up the new language with ease and by the end of year 10 was speaking conversational

Italian almost as well as I could speak Lebanese dialect. I never told my father this of course.

The second time I broke my father's heart was three years later when it was my little brother's turn to start year 9 and he surprised us all by deciding he would also be learning Italian. For me, though, there was no more time for learning fun languages. I was halfway through the HSC, and without any Italian friends to practise with I was already starting to forget much of what I'd learned anyhow. Eventually, all I'll remember are common phrases like *come ti chiami?* What is your name? My Arabic, on the other hand, is finally improving, but this is another thing my father will never know about me.

'You see?' he accused when my brother broke the news. 'This is your doing. Why are my children so ashamed?' Old wounds were opened and for weeks it felt like he couldn't bear to look in my direction.

Come ti chiami? Come mi chiamo? What is my name?

I don't think I can tell you about the third time I broke my baba's heart after all but maybe there is nothing to tell other than there was no fourth time.

Elias Jahshan is an editor and freelance writer based in London. He was born, raised and educated in Sydney with a Lebanese mother and Palestinian father. Before he moved to London in 2016, he was the editor of Star Observer *– Australia's most prolific national LGBT media outlet – for two and a half years. He is the only PoC editor so far in the publication's 40-year history. Elias is also a former board member of Arab Council Australia.*

Coming Out Palestinian

'La!'

Umtoh Fourtoneh's shrill voice rang through the living room. Everyone momentarily diverted their attention from the TV.

'No! They wrong!'

My aunt was berating me for highlighting that Palestine was not on the world map I was looking at. My mum had told me it was right next to Lebanon, where she was from. But I couldn't find Palestine.

'Palestine is real! *N'hna Falasteen!* We are Palestinian!' Umtoh said, wagging her finger at me. 'Never, ever forget.'

I was about seven at the time. Now thirty-four, I can still vividly recall my aunt's passionate words. It's my earliest memory of becoming aware of the concept of being Palestinian. My earliest memory of learning where my family is from. It's also my earliest memory of feeling some of the epigenetic trauma that my aunt, my late dad and all their cousins endured in 1948.

The birth of my Palestinian identity came well before my adolescence, a period that saw the birth of another concept intersecting with my culture: my sexuality. But it took a few more years before I felt pride in being Palestinian – and gay. I endured a period of questioning my sense of self. I had to navigate boundaries seemingly defined for me not just by predominantly white Australia but also from within my own community.

Before pride, I had to endure a period of shame. I went through a series of experiences that spiralled and repeated themselves. Before pride, I first had to come out as a Palestinian. For it wasn't until I felt pride in being Palestinian that my coming-out journey as a gay man truly began.

*

'So, do you like throwing stones?'

The mustard I was squeezing from a dispenser missed a spot over the toasted buns. I was brought to a momentary halt. The shift manager chuckled as he turned to place a batch of patties on the grill.

The question, which he asked during one of my Friday night shifts at McDonald's in Macquarie Centre, pertained to talk about my 'nationality'. I had told him I was born and raised in Sydney, but my mother was Lebanese and my dad Palestinian.

I don't exactly remember what I said in response to his question. But I do remember not raising my eyes. I just carried on preparing the cheeseburgers, ignoring the inexplicable humiliation rising from the pit of my stomach. I tried assuring myself the manager was joking. That it was just harmless banter. That it wasn't supposed to be a big deal.

I was only fifteen.

I didn't understand it at the time, but what I felt was shame. The manager's casually racist, mocking question was defined by a simplistic view of my cultural identity. I was made to feel inferior, and unwittingly accepted it.

He was certainly not alone in his homogeneous, skewed view of Palestinians. The incident occurred when news headlines were dominated by the second intifada. There was hardly any nuance, and historic revisionism was rife – especially in Australia's parochial media. More than anything, Palestinians were denied agency to tell their stories.

As a result, western media often portrayed the Israeli military as the 'goodies'. Israel's democracy and European immigrant influence suited the west's proclivities too. It wasn't otherised, even though Jewish culture has much in common with Levantine Arab culture, and even though Hebrew and Arabic share linguistic roots. The ongoing human rights abuses and racist policies inflicted by countless Israeli governments were excused – or worse yet, justified. Palestinians protesting on the streets, often throwing stones at Israeli tanks, made us look barbaric and violent through western media lens. We weren't just otherised – we were the 'baddies'.

*

As a teenager I suppressed my Palestinian identity outside family circles. There were times when I'd forget, like that shift at McDonald's, but I'd always regret it. It wasn't just because I feared being associated with stereotypes. I was bogged down by an incessant feeling of otherness or being judged whenever I did disclose my background.

I was constantly met with the ignorant 'you're what?' or 'where's that?' reactions, or the 'you're fair for a Palestinian' remark, as if my skin colour required validation for white consumption. Or worse yet, the 'Palestine doesn't exist' comment and the 'what do you think of Israel?' question, designed to entrap and prove that we are (somehow) innately anti-Semitic.

How people viewed my Palestinian identity put me in a state of perpetual worry of being outcast if I inadvertently said the wrong thing. It felt like a curse. It'd be easy to blame it on my teenage naivety, but in retrospect it was shame that held me back. My self-worth depended on the approval of white Australia, which had seemingly set the parameters of my identity. The shame I felt subsequently allowed those parameters to define me.

Instead of lying outright, I developed a habit of only disclosing my Lebanese heritage. At least the language is the same and the cultural similarities endless. Even at high school where a chunk of my grade were students of Lebanese background – it was in the Parramatta area, after all – the majority never knew about my Palestinian side. Ironically, I still had to deal with Lebanese stereotypes, especially when gang violence in south-west Sydney dominated headlines in the late 1990s early 2000s.

At home it was a different story. Countless evenings in the lounge room, around the dinner table and even car drives were spent with my father and me talking about Palestine and Israel. Dad would also recall his happy childhood in Jaffa, of the beachside home in the Ajami neighbourhood that he, his sister and widowed mother lived in with his uncle and cousins. He'd reminisce about the taste of Jaffa's legendary oranges, how the Ottoman clock tower in the town centre was a popular meeting spot, and long summers spent by the beach. He'd also recount Orthodox Easter 1948, when his family fled Jaffa amidst invading Zionist troops. How they all squeezed on the back of a truck with barely any personal belongings and headed to Ramallah. And how, en route, they were stopped by Zionist troops who forced Muslims out and made them 'spit' on the Prophet Mohammed, while Christians like my dad's family looked on, paralysed by fear.

Dad was only nine and a half when the Nakba began, but the experience was seared into his memory right up until he died in 2009. He was never able to shake off the trauma of dispossession and loss of homeland. It became a sorrowful and significant part of my family's history and identity.

Millions of Palestinians – whether they live within Israeli borders, the West Bank and Gaza, or among the global diaspora – live with their own unique family inheritance.

It is a legacy of loss and despair, of painful and bittersweet memories. Anger at consistently having the legitimacy of our culture, history and our families questioned. And exhaustion for being forced to validate ourselves as human beings.

This epigenetic experience also lives in the deep, collective yearning for justice we carry in our bodies, especially since the Nakba continues today. My dad Faris, his sister Fourtoneh and all their cousins are shining examples of this – and everyone in my generation has inherited it.

While I had no problems living and embracing my culture at home, Dad never knew I avoided acknowledging my Palestinian identity in public. Neither did my mum, Georgette. I wish they did, though – especially Dad. I'd do anything for him to be here again, even if he just berated me for not standing up for myself. To remind me no-one has a right to tarnish our Palestinianness through sweeping, simplistic assumptions or stereotypes. He would've lectured me on why visibility is important, and why we should never allow our history and culture to be revised or erased. Most importantly, he would have instilled me with pride.

*

My earliest memory of standing firm on my Palestinian identity occurred when I was sixteen – in the immediate aftermath of 9/11, of all things. Throughout school I had itinerant teachers – support tutors for students who were hard of hearing, like myself. I saw them once a week during my free periods and they often played the role of middleman with my regular teachers.

'Those Palestinians will not stop until they get what they bloody want.'

It saddens me that this was uttered by one of those itinerant teachers during a chat in one of our sessions post 9/11. This kind teacher who I had had since year 7 had suddenly shown her true colours. However, my conscience was stirred.

'I'm actually half Palestinian,' I responded.

'Oh? But you're not Muslim?'

What followed was an engaging discussion. I told her a bit about my family and how Palestinians are not defined by religion. But I don't know if my attempt to humanise led her to acknowledge our dignity. I was too young to notice, and by the end of that year I had a new itinerant teacher anyway.

Nonetheless, the incident was a turning point.

Earlier that year I had started taking part in public speaking as an extracurricular activity. I initially did it to prove to myself that I didn't need to start speech therapy again, given my hearing loss and the way puberty blues was affecting my self-confidence and diction. But it became more than that.

Dad was floored when he watched me at the first competition, where my speech argued that Australia's multiculturalism depended on being a metaphoric salad bowl, rather than the implied assimilation of a melting pot. I didn't win, but the joy in Dad's face as he eagerly patted my back and fought an obvious urge to hug me in front of my peers made me feel like a winner.

In the final school term, several weeks after 9/11, I competed in another competition. My dad came along again, this time even more enthusiastic. My speech was about Palestine and Israel, interspersed with the metaphor of a boxing ring where Yasser Arafat and Ariel Sharon engaged in an endless, exhausting fight with no winner.

I remember Dad beaming with pride afterwards. 'You should've seen his speech!' he exclaimed to Mum once we were home. That speech was a pivotal moment for me, even if Dad didn't see it that way. It was essentially the first time I came out as a Palestinian in a public space. It felt liberating – although that feeling was fleeting. This was in the wake of 9/11 after all, when racism towards Arabs escalated. It still took a few more years before I came full circle, but there was no turning back from here.

*

When the burden of questioning myself as a Palestinian started to lift, I unwittingly created more room for the confusion around my sexuality. I lied profusely to myself about being gay. I could hardly be blamed. In most Arab families, personal success is measured by marriage and children before career or academic success. The stigmatisation of gay relationships is prevalent, and most Arab countries criminalise homosexuality. In a few extreme cases it's punishable by death.

I grew up in a part of Sydney that had no visible gay community at the time, and within a culture that is unfortunately rampant with hypermasculinity and toxic patriarchy. I had cousins and family friends who'd make gay men the subject of homophobic jokes. I only ever heard 'that's gay' used in derogatory contexts, and boys were expected to act or have 'masculine' interests otherwise they'd be mocked or belittled.

Family is everything in Arab culture, and I was racked with anxiety over being outcast if I ever came out or 'got caught' – even if it was as simple as someone walking into my bedroom as I watched *Queer as Folk* on SBS. I worried I could ruin my parents' upstanding reputation in family circles for having a gay son and becoming the subject of gossip. But more than anything, I feared being excommunicated by my parents.

It didn't help that I was crippled with fear about how Dad would react. He once responded to a question of mine with a cold stare, declaring I'd no longer be his son if I were gay. I was only seventeen. It hurts that this memory is seared into my mind, alongside others where he mocked gay men. It forces me to reconcile the fact Dad had faults – just like any other human being – when all I want to do is remember him as my hero. It wasn't entirely his fault, though. He was of a different generation, where the cultural stigma around homosexuality was even deeper than it is now. I have long forgiven him.

When I started coming out at age twenty, my siblings and close cousins advised me not to tell my parents at all. I wasn't ready anyway. However, things changed when I spent a year studying abroad in France in 2007. During that year I turned twenty-two. Away from family, I backpacked through Europe and embarked on a journey of self-discovery. I accepted my sexuality was as much a part of me as my culture, as my severe hearing loss. I found fulfilment in navigating all identities as they intersected. I started to feel comfortable in my own skin – not just a gay man, but a gay Arab deaf man. I grew exponentially.

Once back in Sydney, there were times when I felt suffocated. Despite my liberating year abroad, I just wasn't ready to come out to my parents. I also had to finish my final year of university. When Dad was in hospital and had just weeks to live, my older sister asked if I was going to come out to him. I remember responding with a resounding no. I couldn't risk jeopardising my relationship with him when he was at his most vulnerable.

I've since made peace with that decision. It ensured he and I were on good terms when he departed this world. Amidst the grief – a grief I've never been able to shake off, and probably never will – I was lucky to have had the closure of telling him I loved him before he died. But if I did come out to him, I know the conversations we could've had would have changed his views, even if it took time. After all, Dad was progressive for his generation, and he often said my happiness was more important than his.

It took a couple more years before I came out to Mum and Umtoh. I was dating someone at the time, and my siblings and close cousins were becoming jittery after being cornered in conversations with extended family members where – for some reason – my love life was the topic. They encouraged me to tell Mum and Umtoh, on the basis it was better they heard it from me before any chance of gossip started. I agreed. Suffice to say, neither conversation was easy.

While my mum's and aunt's journeys to acceptance are still far from over, it was the last major obstacle in my coming-out journey. Free from most of the anxiety and fears that kept me in the closet before, I found myself pursuing a lifestyle of revelry as if to make up for lost time as a teenager. I have no regrets – my mid to late twenties were some of the best times in my life.

Mum has come a long way, though. When I first came out to her she refused to meet my then boyfriend. She refused to revisit the topic altogether. She was in denial (as was my aunt). But when I became editor of *Star Observer,* Mum quietly congratulated me. There was also an incident where she spoke of watching an interview on Arabic satellite TV of Omar Sharif Junior and how his family – including his famous Hollywood grandfather – reacted to his coming out as gay. Seven years later, after I had moved to London and Mum visited, she met Aaron. I would go on to marry him in a civil ceremony, and she now asks about him during our weekly FaceTime. Things are still far from perfect, but I've never been as liberated as I am today.

*

At my host university in Caen, France, there was a fellow international student, a Palestinian, who inspired me. At the end of one of our classes, as students were rushing out to enjoy the fresh snow, he took his time to lay out and fold a black and white patterned scarf on his desk. With an air of confidence, he wrapped the scarf around his neck and walked out, his head held high. I realised he had adorned himself in a keffiyeh – and I wanted to do the same.

Around this time, the keffiyeh was all the rage in the west. Fast fashion retailers were mass-producing knock-offs in various colours. A significant cultural motif for Palestinians had been reduced to a 'stylish' or 'edgy' fashion statement. It was blatant cultural appropriation. If people were going to see me with one, it had to be authentic. My dad agreed – but he never lived to see that.

He was seventy when he died, having lived in Australia for more than forty years. He never had the chance to revisit Jaffa, not since 1948. I had promised him I'd 'go back' on his behalf, though. Mum and I made a holiday of it, starting in Lebanon before visiting Dad's cousins in Amman and Jerusalem. I was twenty-six at the time, the same age he was in 1964 when he left Amman – where he, Umtoh and most of their extended family ended up after 1948. His cousins kept telling me I looked so much like him. Some never saw him again after he left for Sydney. In their memories he is an eternal twenty-six year old.

In Jaffa, I imagined a younger version of Dad wandering the streets. I stopped by the church where the last photo of him and my aunt was taken on Orthodox Palm Sunday 1948. I attempted, but failed, to locate the grave of my grandfather – who died months after Dad was born – at a cemetery atop a cliff overlooking the Mediterranean. I also found a cleared block of land which, according to a map I was given by one of Dad's cousins in Amman, was likely to have been where his childhood home stood by the beach in Ajami. Dad's presence was everywhere. It was bittersweet.

I also had a few daytrips to the West Bank. At a market stall in Bethlehem, I finally bought an authentic keffiyeh – one made by Hirbawi, the last family-run Palestinian scarf business.

I often think about this trip, how much it changed me. The keffiyeh I purchased became a symbol of my journey since I was a teenager. I had finally come full circle as a Palestinian. I continue to wear that keffiyeh any chance I have, usually in winter. It's a tribute to my Palestinian heritage, a symbol of solidarity, and a visual reminder we exist and that our culture and history is real. It is empowering and liberating.

I also wear it in honour of Dad, who I miss dearly. Not a day goes by where I don't wish he was around to have seen me grow into the man I am today. A man who overcame shame to be able to navigate being proudly gay and proudly Palestinian with ease. A man who I hope, in turn, would make him proud.

Here, at Home

I don't have my father's tongue
I possess my mother's belt
In my mouth
I choose my words carefully
Soft leather that holds will wield bruises
When whipped with cruelty
I don't have my mother's eyes
But I own his look with the arched hazel wit
That fills the outside with crows and lines
We borrow the same faces
With the same phrases
But I'm left with the aftertaste of the English translations
As he pirouettes in Arabic; I envy his ease
Wishing he taught me the smooth dervish rotations of
Gutter slang with Quranic verse; the secrets of digging
Up the dirt to explore the root of a word

Lam. Meem. Seen.

No melting *3asal* falls from my lips
to soften the streets with sweet talk
Just halting guttural stops stuck
Like honey between my fingers
Thick and warm with memories
Of never learning to speak

So I steal from the beehive
To sugar-coat this poem
I salute with his big nose in defiance
Of the small and upturned
With my hair in his dark curls
Against the straight and the straw
But as I peel and burn and slip
Off the layers of the skin that freckles
Fades and wrinkles

I remember

I live on borrowed time on stolen land
With a melanin content not quite designed for this sun
A colony has many fingers, and my ancestors are 163 years
Of soil pinched between pointer and thumb
Pretending there is no dirt under our nails
I look at
my hands to see them rusted with the red ochre of blood

Wu'du washes me clean enough to link into a steadying grip
An elbow of three for the time it took to learn
That I can stand foot to foot with the call to resistance
And I bear witness to the scars of a racist past with scars of the racism
That has passed through my body;
I'm tired of trading in tokens that distort us into clarity,
Seeking truth, I found it cannot find a place to fit
Between the unfixed myths
Of terra nullius and Other

I might have a
Displaced face looped in spelling mistakes
With cursive cursed letters from a father in *Tora*
A disoriented coloniser I call my mother
Who holds with one hand and belts with the other

I etched love into my shoulder

To let them know I have nothing else to offer
Nowhere else to go
Never having known anywhere except
This stitched-up body and sentimental soul
Stranded on an island
Here, at home.

3asal: honey
Wu'du: Islamic ritual wash to cleanse before prayer
Tora: one of the major prisons in Cairo, Egypt

Growing up mixed race and Muslim, with an Egyptian father and an Australian mother, came with a set of experiences that shaped a feeling of disorientation in the world of being neither 'here nor there'. This poem attempts to capture the tangled threads that make up my relationships to land, body, history and faith.

***Lamisse Hamouda** is an Australian-Egyptian poet, writer, youth worker and human rights activist. In 2018, her father was wrongfully imprisoned in Cairo after arriving for a holiday. Lamisse led a campaign for his freedom, and he was finally released after 405 days behind bars.*

***Sara El Sayed** is an Egyptian-born freelance writer and Master of Fine Arts student based in Brisbane. Her research focus is digital storytelling by migrant Egyptian women. Her work, both fiction and non-fiction, is influenced by her culture, her family and her identity as a migrant.*

Aerobics for Arabs

'Just do it, quickly, before Mama gets back,' I told my little sister Aisha, thrusting the Nair hair-removal bottle into her hand as she sat on the couch. 'Cover my whole back.' She pressed the nozzle, white foam oozing out onto the provided pink sponge. She spread it from the small of my back, across my shoulders, up to the point my neck met my hairline.

'Is it burning yet?' she asked, frosting me like a sheet of brownies. She kept one eye on the television. It was *The Simpsons*. Bart had offended the Australians and had to apologise to the nation by receiving a booting to the behind.

'No,' I lied. I could feel it turning red.

'Why do they think Australians talk like that? Do we talk like that?' she said. The foam was bubbling. On the screen, Bart pulled down his pants and mooned an angry mob. *Don't tread on me* read the words written on his bottom.

*

Since starting school in Australia, all I wanted was to be on the aerobics team. We didn't have aerobics back in Egypt. We had ballet. I tried it. Hated it. I wasn't delicate enough. But aerobics – that was a dance with grit. The girls were fit and sporty. They were strong, too. You could see it in the way they held themselves solid in their push-ups, and the way their legs flew into the air, to limits that seemed humanly impossible, and stayed there. Every movement was firm and resolute.

I wanted everything to do with aerobics. I wanted the blue and white sequined leotard with matching scrunchie. I wanted the stockings that made your legs three shades darker than the rest of your body. I wanted the white tube socks and I wanted the Princess Reebok shoes.

So, in grade 6 I decided to try out.

'It's compulsory,' I whispered to myself, practising with my bedroom door closed. I had to develop a convincing argument if my parents were to ever let me do it. 'It's part of an exam at school.' No. That could easily be disproved. 'My friends said that if I don't do it they won't be my friends anymore.' No. They'd never believe that. None of my friends participated in competitive aerobics. And even if my parents did believe it, they wouldn't care.

Mama was in the kitchen washing up after *aasha*. Her bracelets jangled in the sink. I picked up a plate and scrubbed.

'What do you want?' she said, eyeing the plate that had already been cleaned.

'I'm just helping,' I said. Mama dried her hands on the tea towel and proceeded to put dishes in the cupboard. 'I was just wondering . . .'

'Yes?' she said.

'I was just wondering if I could do some dancing at school.'

'Dancing? I thought you didn't like ballet.'

'I don't. This is different. It's a sporty-dance. You do it in teams and you compete against other teams. Like basketball. But dancing.'

'I've never heard of it.'

'Everyone here does it.'

'Do they?'

I nodded. 'Please, Mama.'

'I don't know. Have you asked your father?'

'It's just the try-out. I probably won't even get in. I just want to try.'

Mama closed the cupboard door and looked at me. 'Have you done your homework?'

'No. Not yet.'

'So, am I supposed to let you do this basketball dancing while you fail school?'

'It's not basketball dancing. It's aerobics. Competitive sport aerobics. And I always do my homework. I promise I will get all As if you let me try out. Please.'

Mama sighed and flicked the kettle on.

The next day I walked into the school hall, placed my signed note on the table and sat down with the other students. The place was absolutely packed. They never turned kids away from the sport, everyone got put on a team, basically. But for the competitive girls, it was a matter of *which* team they got on.

But I didn't really care. I was there. And I was going to be an aerobics girl.

The teacher was crouched on stage, fiddling with a CD player. A sped-up version of *Chain Reaction* by Diana Ross played quietly through the speakers. She looked frustrated, taking the disc out and blowing on it, rubbing it on her nylon tracksuit.

Wires crackled and suddenly the song boomed through the PA system. Kids covered their ears. The teacher hit stop. The hall erupted with laughter.

'Alright, that's enough,' she said, adjusting her pants as she stood up. 'We have a lot of you here and only forty-five minutes to get through this, so everyone needs to be quiet and cooperative.'

The teacher beckoned to the side of the stage. Out jogged Jess and Gina, their straight, long ponytails flipping as they moved. Their freckled skin made them look like they were cut from the same piece of fabric. They took their positions on stage. Gina on the floor in a straddle, hands on hips. Jess standing behind her, fingers splayed in jazz hands over her face, palms to the audience. The teacher hit play.

Bing! An alien sound effect started the song. The girls swung into motion, making sharp movements with their limbs. Star jumps. High kicks. Push-ups. Splits. All peppered with saturated facial expressions. Grins. Winks. Kisses. I couldn't help but smile back at them.

The teacher hit stop. 'Okay, everyone up.'

*

I confronted my parents in the living room, holding the flyer tight in my hand. It crumpled more with every sweaty moment. On it was a picture of last year's team winning a state competition in their sparkly leotards. Jess and Gina front and centre. It only took a glimpse of it for Baba to make his decision.

'She's not to do it,' he said, picking the TV remote up. Aisha was watching *The Simpsons.*

'*Eat my shorts,*' said Bart, before Baba changed the channel. Aisha shot him an angry look and left the room.

'End of discussion,' he said, leaning back in the reclining chair as the Arabic news blared. The beads of his *sibha* clicked together in his hand.

'But I want to. I got in. I have to.'

'You're not going to.'

'It's not that bad,' I said, re-examining the flyer.

'Good girls don't dance around on stage in their underwear,' he said.

'It's not underwear, it's a uniform. I have to wear it if I'm part of the team.' I looked over at Mama. She looked sorry for me.

'What if you wear something over the top? Some trousers? Your tracksuit is nice,' she said.

I was about to cry. 'I can't wear trousers. I'll look stupid.'

'Well, maybe if you wear trousers,' Baba said.

I didn't get the Reebok shoes. Payless white sneakers had to do. But I got the dark brown stockings.

'Please don't make me wear trousers,' I pleaded with Mama as she looked through the clothing racks in Target. She picked out a pair of black, mid-thigh bike shorts. A compromise.

'You can't go out on stage wearing nothing,' she said.

I sighed as we headed for the checkout. 'The list says I need foundation too.'

'No,' she said.

*

The teacher opened up a cardboard box at our first rehearsal. It was full of leotards. They looked like they were made from the skin of mermaids. I couldn't wait to try mine on.

'Once you find your size,' said the teacher, 'you're to sign your leo out, then take it home. You are to take care of it. Wash it gently by hand, with cold water. If I hear of any machine washing, you will be sorry.' She stepped aside as the sea of girls rushed for the box.

I grabbed what I could – what I thought looked like my size. I went into the bathroom and pulled it on. It was slightly too tight, but I could live with it. I stepped out of the cubicle to get a good look at myself in the bathroom mirror. The straps dug into my shoulders a bit, but other than that I felt on top of the world. My legs looked long and brown, my torso covered in glitter. I was an aerobics girl. Finally.

I dreaded the thought of covering it all with the shorts Mama bought.

'Oh my God,' said a voice from behind me. In the mirror I saw Jess and Gina, gawking. A group of girls around them giggled. 'Do you guys see that?' I turned around. They were all looking at me.

'So gross,' said Gina. 'What are you, an ape?'

'Your back is so hairy,' said Jess. 'You look really bad in that leo.'

'You need to shave yourself,' said Gina.

I ran back into the toilet stall. I didn't come out until the bell rang.

*

Aisha wiped the foam away with a damp cloth. With it came small brown flecks of hair.

'You're all red,' she said.

'Where?'

'Everywhere. Should I get Mama?'

'No.'

'Does it hurt?'

'No.'

I sped to the shower and ran cold water over my welts. It was heaven. I dried myself, pulled on my stockings, my leotard, and bike shorts over the top.

Mama dropped me off in the car park outside the competition hall.

'Don't you dare take those shorts off,' she said through the window.

'I won't,' I said. My back was still stinging.

It was our very first performance. Backstage the smell of hairspray filled the air. The music being played in the auditorium boomed through the walls. I stood at a mirror to fix my flyaways.

'Wow, looks like the woolly mammoth went to the barber,' said Jess. Her bun was pulled back so tight I could see a vein bulging from her forehead.

Gina walked over and eyed me up and down, her mascara-clad eyelashes flapping like thick spider legs. 'Nice shorts,' she said, Jess giggling next to her, 'but you might want to check your stockings.'

I turned to look. A ladder ran up my calf. I sighed.

'That's what you get when you buy your costume from the Reject Shop,' said Gina. They both laughed.

'I never liked the colour anyway,' I said, pretending not to care. I walked over to the curtained changing area.

'Neither do I, really,' said Jess. 'Looks like poo.' I closed the curtain behind me. I could feel their breath through the material. 'But don't worry, your legs are about the same colour anyway. No-one will notice.' They both laughed again.

To take my stockings off I had to take off my shoes, then my socks, then my shorts, then my leotard. When it came to putting my shorts back on, I stopped. None of the other girls wore shorts. I didn't understand what was so different about me. That I had to wear them and they didn't.

Mama wouldn't know if I left them off. I rolled them up into a small ball and held them tightly in my fist. When I emerged from the changing area, the teacher was standing on the other side of the curtain.

'You'd better hurry yourself. All the other girls are ready. Why isn't your makeup on?' she asked.

'I don't have any makeup.'

The teacher huffed and walked away.

'She can borrow some of my makeup, Miss,' said Jess from behind me. I felt a cold, wet sponge being drawn along my back. I twisted to see a slash of ivory foundation across my skin.

'Much better!' said Jess. She and Gina laughed.

'Leave me alone,' I said, trying to reach to wipe it off.

'*Leave me alone,*' they mocked in unison.

I dropped my arms. My fists clenched. I wanted to hit them. I felt the ball of material press into my palm. I clenched and clenched until it felt hard like a rock. The girls were still laughing as they walked away.

I followed them, raising my hand.

'Hey!' I shouted. They turned around.

I pegged my shorts as hard as I could. They shot right into Jess's face.

She stepped back, shocked. Then started to cry. 'I'm telling!' she said, before calling out to the teacher. 'Miss! Miss! Help! She attacked us!'

Gina looked at her friend, mouth wide open. I wished I had a second pair to hurl.

Eat my shorts.

Yassir Morsi is a lecturer in Politics at La Trobe University and researches how creative non-fiction can address global violence and the question of diversity.

Ros Bil Laban

1.

'Jimmy' had a ritual when he picked me up from the airport. He hummed *tun ta ra ra run* and waited for my *tun tun*. It made sure it was really me, he joked. I'd then feel his stubble on my boyish cheeks as he squeezed his salaams into me. I'd smell the Cleopatra cigarettes, his leather jacket and overdone cologne 'three 5s'. It gave me a headache, but it all signalled a return home to Egypt.

Gamal, or Jimmy as we called him, had a huge heart. May Allah have mercy on him. It is somewhat sadly poetic that my uncle died of dilated cardiomyopathy – his heart literally became too big. My tearful aunties fought to explain why he died so young. Mona says it was the smokes and the many spoons of sugar in his tea. Shosho says it was work and the hardships of poverty. And Gigi lamented how corruption and the country's broken promises broke his heart. All are killers of the working-class Arab.

2.

When I first came to Australia, I felt I had to perform Aladdin for classmates at primary school for them to like me. I put on accents and spoke about my pet camel back home. I felt enslaved to live up to stereotypes, as opposed to having to break them. High school wasn't much better. I was just a wog or the nephew of Saddam Hussein.

When I was eight Tom, my friend in class, told us all we should blow up the whole 'Middle East'. It's a 'bloody mess'. I protested. 'My family lives there. My cousins, aunties and my uncles. My grandmother. They are not messy at all!'

After school I ran home to Dad and tried to convince him that we had to do something. I had a plan too. I told him that with all the urgency he could muster to call his mum and get her to send Tom some *ros bil laban* (rice pudding). My dad wasn't interested. Instead, he spread two fingers into the shape of a V and punched it towards the ceiling. Basically, he instructed me how to respond to my friend. I did not appreciate his advice, and the next time I saw Dad he was taking off his belt, his wide eyes, as I scurried through the kitchen, slipping on the rice and milk I had spilt on the floor.

Despite having no rice pudding to prove our worth, the next day I negotiated with Tom. I promised him a tasty dessert in return for him not calling for genocide out loud. He felt reluctant to give up the right but promised if the dessert was as good as I claimed he would when he was president not blow up that part of the Middle East where my family lived. The schoolyard negotiation lasted for five minutes. I didn't know then but talking to white boys about the value of Arab lives would become a lifetime vocation.

I remember that night I told the story to Uncle Jimmy on a crackling phone. 'What's wrong?' he quizzed. I felt embarrassed. But after a few repeats of saying '*alhamdulillah*' and 'nothing' I eventually burst. I hadn't defended my people, I cried. He responded with a roaring laugh and told me not to worry. Arab leaders had sold us for far less than a promise of *Sito*'s *ros bil laban.*

Perhaps all these complexities and guilt that reside within me help explain why, as an adult, a compulsion to break free from being this or that type of their Arab persists. But this will to shape my fingers into a V didn't come until my undergraduate years.

I remember when my impatience finally found its words. After all those years, and eleven tiring weeks of studying European thinkers, my course provided but two hours to investigate my people, my world and my history. Week twelve of 'Politics in our Time' was on terrorism. Thus, the recommended readings, providing background, were all about the Muslim world. Well, really, it was all about the Arab world, which the professor called the Muslim world. I remember how all week leading up to class I felt a mistrust in my ability. A stifling pressure to know more than my classmates suffocated me. I felt I had to speak because I was the native. I was to be Aladdin again. The pressure to be more informed gripped me and turned me insecure. I read the prescribed texts twice, and then again, and then again on the morning of the class. My eyes focused on every word, searching for error or for hope.

I know now of the pervasive racism which compels people of colour to defend their traditions and themselves. But perhaps I will never learn why we bother to begin with. For, during class, chatty students knew little and cared less. They knew nothing about the pressure I felt, or why I remained silent for the first half of class. I sat there listening to white chitter-chatter, as terrorism, Islam and the Arab world mixed with their entitlement to produce stereotype and error. Confidence matched ignorance as opinions sold themselves as facts. The longer the class went, the louder a nagging voice within me pushed me to yell. I could feel the side stares of students, as if they were asking me whether I would talk, or whether I agreed with their overpriced points. But it was something else that made me talk.

My classmate Andy was berating the Arab world for its lack of democracy. 'If I were Arab,' he said, 'I would complain less about the West . . .' And, just like that, with little control, I yelled, 'But, mate, you're not an Arab!' I sounded so territorial, angry, and a little out of control. It is a strange feeling to feel like you are their stereotype.

I mention this memory not because of Andy or my anger or that I finally spoke, but because of what took place in the following days. Initially my private thoughts on the way out of class tried to justify my outburst. I reasoned that I had only tried to explain that Andy could not abstract being Arab and say 'If I were . . .' You had to hear about the tragedies and the triumphs from uncles and aunties and have their emotions run through your veins like their blood. You must embody the pain of hearing about '48, '67, and feel the triumph of '73; before you know why or how you feel what you feel as an Arab. But these internal justifications would haunt me, for their truths also felt distant to me, and soon enough my own words would turn me inside out.

The next day, still angered by Andy, awake for *fajr* (morning prayer), I promised myself to learn more, to know more, to call my uncles and aunties, to connect, to get closer to Islam. I would learn about all the wars and the oppression and resilience. I wanted to speak with fluency, feel the fluency, and close the gap between my identity and my culture. And, then halfway through this promise, I stared into the floor, I missed Jimmy.

3.

I must have been five, maybe six. Jimmy and I spent a whole morning making a kite. It was a beautiful Alexandrian day with a pale blue sky and a mild breeze. I watched our kite glide in circles, scared to ask for my turn. Jimmy knew. He got on a knee and gave me the string. Whatever happens, he told me, hold on tight.

After only a minute, a powerful gust of wind took the kite out of my young hands. It flew off flapping, as if laughing. Jimmy shook his head with a wry smile. I whimpered a tearful apology as my uncle placed his hand on my shoulder. Staring at the vanishing kite, with my uncle's hand on my shoulder, I heard him tell me, 'It's lost forever, *khalas habibi, kheir*, everything is meant to be. It's *naseeb*'. I never understood the pain behind his words 'lost forever' until he died years later.

4.

While on my knees in morning prayer, in the dark, my tired eyes stared at the line of light. One slither of dawn snuck beneath my bedroom door. It was too early, and I should have taken the hint I was not yet ready. As I stood up onto my feet and lifted my two hands to whisper, '*Allahu Akbar*', I paused. I could feel the concern rising through my throat. I ignored it and recited the *al-Fatihah*. I moved on to the next surah. I had barely memorised it, and it was one where I did not know the words, just its sounds. As I recited, I could hear my broken Arabic cut the roof of my mouth. Almost intuitively, I heard myself say the same thing I had said to Andy. 'But mate, you're not an Arab.'

5.

Sometime after that incident in the class, as part of my commitment to being more Arab, I decided I would spend my morning making *ros bil laban*. It was my favourite dessert growing up. My *sito* made it for me when I was little, may Allah have mercy on her. As a happy grandson I would stuff my face with spoonful after spoonful. The whole family knew the fridge lined up with plates and small bowls of *ros bil laban* was for Yassir. It was an exciting occasion when *Sito* prepared it for me. I was slight, but I lugged a dining room chair to the stove so I could stand over her shoulder as she cooked. Watching with anticipation, I'd direct her to make more. And between the sweet whiff of steaming milk and rosewater, we chuckled at the rest of the family's jealousy. For only she and I knew the secret recipe.

Perhaps for this reason, as an adult, I supposed I could make the dessert by myself. I was confident I didn't need a recipe, only a dining room chair. I placed it next to me at the stove as a symbolic gesture to reconnect to my grandmother, to relive the sweet memory.

I will spare you the details of what happened next. But by the end of the day all I managed was a burned pot. The pot I chose was too small. I struggled to save it by pouring it into another pot, but a lot of milk had already spilled when boiling over. Now I had run out, so I tried to use water instead. The final humiliation came when my sister's dog refused to taste what I had made. Scrubs stared up at me with pitiful eyes almost hiding behind the fallen dining room chair.

Really, the attempt works as a metaphor for so much of my aims of connecting with my heritage: the will is there but the know-how isn't.

Watching the Netflix series *Mysteries of the Nile* (*Grand Hotel* in Arabic) with my wife came with another burn. She is not Arab, but she speaks better Arabic than me. As part of the Eritrean diaspora, she grew up in Sudan. While eating *lib* and drinking sweet red tea, she asked me to come and watch the show with her. I refused and made some glib political point. The cause of all Arab problems, I claimed, came back to Egyptian and Arab TV's love for exaggeration. Besides, I had to finish my essential dialogue between Badiou and Žižek. But, while trying to read, I could hear the Egyptian dialect, and it made me want to taste the *lib* and the sweet tea. I was drawn in. I lost my book sometime before my hand reached for the *lib*. For one beautiful moment I returned home, I could feel my uncle's stubble on my cheeks. I missed my people, my heart was warm. I could smell boiling milk and rosewater.

My wife and I binged on the show. We went through thirty-odd episodes in two and a half days. During one episode I laughed at a joke and my wife gave me a strange look. I ignored her as I tried to crack the *lib* with my front teeth, but I just ended up eating the whole thing. Then my wife laughed heartily at a joke and I didn't. She very kindly put the English subtitles on.

I reason that these moments result from living abroad. I reason being Arab 'runs in my blood', so my delighted grandparents told me. A few weeks after I was born my parents sent me back to Egypt. *Sito* brought me up on her shoulder and love. My uncles competed for my attention and Jimmy won. I spent the first years of my childhood among a score of smoking uncles and pampering aunts. There were the usual dramas and heartbreaks and constant fighting and wonderful bursts of laughter we shared.

I was their first grandchild. A source of family pride, I was their future because Dad was the only one of eight sons who had escaped abject poverty. He got a scholarship to study in the UK where I was born, and going back to Egypt every year, I would hear stories about how he studied under street lights when electricity at home got cut.

I remember how every Friday in particular made me feel thrilled to be there together with everyone. On that day, scores of cousins rushed through my grandparents' front door to greet me with laughter and hugs. We would play between the furniture, hiding, running, always smiling. I can still recall the sweet smell of the tangerines and my aunties cutting us guava to share. Only the melodic call to prayer from the local mosque interrupted us.

Although I loved Fridays, they also scared me. When *Gido* first took me to *jummah* it was a big deal. Shosho ironed my *oftan* and *Sito* read prayers over me as she rubbed my shoulder. She placed a *tasbih* in my pocket as Jimmy sprayed a dash of three 5s cologne on my wrists. I smile now. But the mosque at the time brought me some anxiety. All I could do was watch the imam repeat words I didn't understand. He spoke so quickly, and in a version of Arabic I did not know. He seemed angry. As I looked up at *Gido* he sensed my discomfort and whispered softly, 'Just do what I do'.

That night I begged Uncle Jimmy to teach me some Quran.

6.

'I'm serious, I'm not trying to be funny,' I continued over the classroom laughter, staring at Andy. 'What do you know about being Arab?' I remember barely listening to his response. I can recall some murmured reply as he offered an opinion on how he found a chapter he read in the lead-up to the week 'interesting'. The word stayed in the air. It seemed offensive. He was sincere, even somewhat apologetic, but it all felt lazy, it felt like their typical irreverence, a singular but stupid way to describe things: 'interesting'. Because of my scowl, I could feel the class turn against me. I was angry and I had to ask Andy again, I had to say out loud why irritation was just. Of course, I cannot recall every word, but I remember the gist:

> 'You said, if you were Arab? But what would you know? Answer me maybe, what does it mean to lose an uncle to heart failure because he cannot afford the better hospital up the road? Tell me? The hospital made for foreigners and the rich Egyptians you lot feed had his medicine stocked up. What would you know about what it's like for my uncle Mohammad to not be able to rub the oil from work off his hands? It is there permanently, it is there like a tattoo, in his skin, between his nails, in his nostrils. It stamps his tired life as a mechanic since sixteen, for sixteen hours a day. You all sit here sixteen thousand miles away. You speak as if somehow everything is a debate between terrorism and democracy. Forget the bullshit, and the theories and the interesting ideas. What would you know about always wanting to go back to something and it not being there, wishing you had held on a little tighter than you did? What would you know of a life where all

the pain and dislocation and the wars and the walls and the towers . . . and all we have is our own hands on our own shoulders, and all we can tell ourselves after loss is stuff it, *kheir*, it's *naseeb*.'

7.

The kite becomes smaller as if it always moves further away in my memory. I can still hear its flapping sound. No matter how hard I hold on, I know that distance is a tyrant. It is also hard to live in a country that makes that distance felt in different ways. But I have long resolved this, for yes, I am an Arab without being Arabic. I am to borrow the title of this edition, always, and forever, still growing up as an Arab. And over the years it has become more comfortable for me to grow into being my type, with my story, when I own like I owned Andy that day. I am my torn identity, and the edged and jagged bits of its tear, and of an Arabic that cuts my tongue.

So much of my life here in Australia is staring up at a kite and wishing I had held on to it, held on to Jimmy, *Sito*, the smell of guava and every Friday prayer with *Gido*. It gives perspective about the powers of the wind. Distance offers me a way to speak not of loss but of memory. Maybe if I had held on to that kite that day, I would never have remembered what I remember now. For as I write this sentence, I tingle to the warm feel of my uncle's hand on my shoulder. *Naseeb*. And, between writing drafts, I felt compelled. I pulled up a chair from my dining room and dragged it to the kitchen.

It is easier to write for me in a rhizomatic way of disjointed stories because that is my experience of being Arab. Its bits and pieces, flutters, flaps, dances, and in its beauty it resists being held. It is where the wind takes it and I have not lost a kite but forever remembered a blue sky.

The Personal Disclosures of a Young Refugee

They want to hear my story.

I tried to be free. Not as an Australian. Not as an Iraqi. But emancipated as a human.

I was born on August 2000. Named by the UN as the International Year for the Culture of Peace.
While liberation was a grant in the West, we witnessed a 'liberation' corrupted.
A liberation where war never knew its beginning. A liberation where war dreamed of its end.
We were persecuted, truncated, jerked from our roots and our history.
Our Gnostics were marginalised, repressed and massacred.
Our women were kidnapped, raped and beaten.

Discomforts. Guilts. Doubts. Despairs.

Shadows. Smoke. Rifles. Silence. Tassels of blood.

Death was no stranger.

It was an abstract space to be raised in,
one of fragmentation and disjuncture.

Deterrence, detention and denial,
this was the beginning of a 'war on terror'.

But these images aren't for them. This is for me.
I want to be able to tear through my opaque body and witness my own intransigent design over time.

How my sense of freedom was corroded by the sense of my own freedom.
How my sense of justice did me no justice.

I want to know and express.

The sticky taste of fear that coats our tongues.
The panic that gnaws at our insides.
The homesickness for a place that doesn't exist.

The way protest chants roll off my tongue, the way these words feel and the pathos and anger in my voice when exclaiming,

'Say it loud and say it clear, refugees are welcome here!'

I want to understand.

Why we jump through loops of toxic gratitude
Nasty partisan politics
Aligning ourselves with archetypes
Good Refugee. Bad refugee.
Marked by a palpable sense of our own deportability

Our identities pathologised
This is the guise of Australian nationalism.

They want to speak for me.

They who wager our lives, making international compromises and deals
Benighted by ignorance and hate
They who have not been oppressed, not been hungry or broken
They who see us as foreign, suspect and illegal

They only speak of the exceptional among us.

Paragons of human survival.
Economic martyrs
Glorifying those who thrive according to western standards
And dividing the rest.
Spouting intolerance and hate speech
Superfluous words that unweave our humanity at its seams
Commodifying
Aestheticisation
Changing the image seems more important than changing the world

They silence us.

using language as a colonial device
tempering violence
depoliticising
denying our past

refuting our present
leaving in situ dominant neoliberal powers

Who speaks of the barbarity of today and the fear of tomorrow?

That's not all that defines me.
They don't wanna hear my anger, my concerns, my opinions, my perspectives.

I am more than my story,
I am more than a statistic.
I am more than a label,
I am more than a refugee.

I am my ideas, my dreams, my goals, my thoughts, my beliefs.

I'm told it's a privilege in a country where there is no war, no conflict,
But why is this a privilege and not a human right?
I've been told I'm privileged to receive an education,
BUT why is this a privilege and not a human right?
I've been told that I'm privileged to have clothes on my skin,
food on my table and a shelter above my head,
BUT why is this a privilege and not a human right?
I've been told that I'm privileged as a woman to have rights, some power and authority
BUT why is this a privilege and not a universal right?

Mama tells me,
I did not ask to be a refugee, I didn't want to come to your country,

I didn't want to leave my family, I didn't want to lose my house,
I didn't want to start all over again.
I did not come here to get rich or to receive charity,
I did not come here to steal jobs or to cheat the system…
I did not come here by choice.

Baba's silence is our conversation. It tells me everything and nothing.
An alchemist, he made gold.
Conscripted at 16
kidnapped at 36
tasked with the burden of 'survival'
While i, preoccupied with 'self-actualisation'

as I painfully remerged from the canopy of hopelessness, I felt alienated
When i spoke of the body, the psyche, sexuality and the 'spiritual', i felt trivialised
My voice of difference threatened the fragile bonds of my mother culture
My voice of difference threatened the solidarity of my fellow activists

I felt entangled in a generational rebellion against a society that punishes people for moving, for dreaming. How we punished those who were merely seeking a better life.

> *We captured them,*
> *caged them like wild animals,*
> *held them without bail,*
> *relocated them to places inaccessible to legal representation,*
> *and crippled them with political assault.*

Australia, you can't avert and placate the omnipresent spectre of guilt and shame.

Dheyaa
Hamed
Ihab
Rihab
Yahya

(Names of auntie, uncle and cousins lost at sea)

***Rooan Al Kalmashi** completed her Higher School Certificate in 2018 and is currently undertaking an undergraduate degree of Law, Arts in International Studies at the University of Technology. Rooan has been a Youth facilitator for the Global Refugee Consultations (GRYC) working group, a Youth Ambassador for the 20 Voices Leadership program and an ongoing member of the Youth Collective Steering Committee, under Settlement Services International (SSI). Through these roles, she has contributed to a number of advocacy initiatives within the multicultural sector.*

Rawah Arja *is completing her doctorate in Education. She has been shortlisted for the Charlotte Waring Barton Award and is publishing her debut YA novel with Giramondo Publishing. Rawah is a part of Finishing School, a collective of women writers with strong connections to Western Sydney. She was a recipient of the WestWords Varuna Emerging Writers' Residential Program and has featured at Sydney Writers' Festival. Her passion is to write authentic stories that give diverse groups a voice and a sense of belonging and to explore the Muslim identity.*

Single Arab Female

It's the last day of Ramadan and the *Adhan* has been called to break our fast just as the sun sets. My mum is still running around trying to put the last plates of food on the table while the rest of us almost inhale the *fatteh* and *macaroni bi laben*. It's loud and noisy with all thirty of my immediate family members, including my uncle, his wife and their three-year-old daughter, who has a seat reserved on the table that can barely fit the rest of us. My nieces and nephews crawl between our legs and try to sneak some soda drinks while my dad requests an onion just as my mum finally sits down. My sisters yell at their kids to finish their food, though they almost never do, and my brothers talk over each other about some work story that almost got them killed. And just as

I'm about to enjoy myself and relax, the sudden reality of what is about to take place tomorrow dawns on me and my social anxiety like a dark, fraught cloud.

It's Eid al-Fitr, an important religious holiday celebrated by us Muslims worldwide, marking the end of Ramadan, the Islamic holy month of fasting. Eid as a kid was the best time of the year where a day off school was justified and the money I made was mine alone and spent on anything I wanted. I dressed in my finest new clothing, and when I visited people's houses it was my chance to have extra sweets, with my parents too embarrassed to stop me, even after their twenty-minute lecture in the car. But now for people like me, and by that I mean a twenty-nine-year-old single Lebanese woman, it's a time when my inadequacy to find a suitor is at the top of everyone's agenda.

Like most Muslim families, my Eid starts about a week prior, turning the house upside down, cleaning places I never knew existed. From wiping the ceilings and walls, to emptying out the garden shed which stores things my parents refused to throw out. No matter how many times I tried to convince them they didn't need that extra fridge, they always had the same response, 'You Australian kids don't know the value of hard work'. It was much easier to accept that growing up in Australia consequently meant that I had things handed to me, than to go down the road of telling my parents they were full-time hoarders. Plus, I always found it strange that to people like my parents or my cousins overseas, I was considered a full-blown *Aussie* and to some people here I was considered . . . well anything but that.

The need for the house to be completely clean and dust-free has no religious significance yet it takes up most of our time. It's more about what people might think or say or how many people they spread the message to on the Arab hotline. Glass cups and plates with pretty patterns are unpacked and new pot plants are spread around the house. It's the only time our fine china and designer cushions are out for all guests to see.

By now the tables have been cleared and our prayers have been made and I have eaten enough Lebanese sweets to give diabetes a run for its money. It's time for the annual Eid fashion show as all four of my brothers hassle my sisters and me about what outfit they should wear. The youngest, though the biggest of them all, struggles to button his pink, I mean *salmon* coloured shirt, which only prompts my dad to lecture him yet again that if only he'd put as much effort into finding a job as chugging down gallons of protein shakes. I think about what it would be like to put in as much effort into my appearance as my brothers when my brain spots the sweet trays of *ma'amoul* and decides that one last pistachio biscuit can't hurt. My mum stares at me through the window and gives me that look which loosely translates to: *Really? How are you going to fit into your clothes? Remember, you need to look your best if any potential match were to come by.*

It's midnight and the possibility of sleep is here until I discover that my bed is decorated with a million and one fluffy cushions for the traditional house tour my mum gives to showcase her sense of style. If I am going to survive the night, I will have to sleep as though I am paralysed, only using one side of the bed, trying my hardest not to move and ruin the bed display. My eyes shut and the pain in my feet stops till the new day arrives and the festivities of Eid begin. My mum barges into my room, in a panic, yelling that I've slept in and that guests would be here any minute.

It's not even sunrise . . .

I roll out of bed, my eyes still glued together, waiting to use the bathroom when my brothers barge right past me. My mum calls for any clothes to be ironed to be left in the living room; this doesn't include mine because I'm a woman and how dare I not iron my own clothes. I finish getting dressed in clothes that miraculously fit, hours earlier than necessary, and with a face full of the makeup my sisters urged me to put on. 'Don't you want people to notice you?' they both say like that's what someone with social anxiety would crave for: attention. This is the exact time I count the hours till sunset, when my social anxiety and I can slink back to the seclusion of our room and escape people's judgements and the daunting reality of why, oh why, am I still single?

The first guests that arrive are usually close family, like my aunties and uncles and all their *married* children. They know my marital status and only ever make the odd comments like 'This time next year you'll be married' or the 'Don't worry it will happen when you least expect it'. I'm not entirely sure what signals I'm giving out to make people believe that I'm 'worried' or 'expecting' Prince Mohamed to waltz in and sweep me off my feet, but still, I nod and smile and continue to offer sweets.

It continues this way till about midday when there's a break in visitors and it's just my family, all thirty of us. My brothers and sisters give gifts and money to each other's children while my mum rushes to serve lunch, *fasooliya* (beans) and rice, under the vine-leaf pergola. We talk and laugh and my anxiety and I are calm till the next batch of people arrive – *the Fifteen Minutes of Pain Guests.*

These usually consist of Dad's friends of friends, workmates or members of the community who stare and smile while I stare and smile back. Awkward, I know. They proceed to ask my mum questions about my age, occupation and marital status as though I don't exist or as though I can't put two and two together when they drop my name in between their Arabic conversations. My being unwed is not only baffling to them but, for whatever reason, they take it upon themselves to try and figure out why I'm still single, like my life is a game on *Family Feud.*

'Too picky.' 40 points.

'Doesn't give anyone a chance.' 30 points.

'Doesn't put herself out there.' 20 points.

'Has a high standard – needs to shorten her husband checklist.' 10 points. (Who knew having a job or a normal haircut should be negotiable things on a woman's list?)

The intimate details of my personal life are now displayed for all guests, which is about the same time my anxiety searches for different escape exits. 'But why?' they ask over and over again, and more than anything I want to say, *Because the sons you raise are not husband or father material,* but I stay quiet and smile through my teeth, praying that by some miracle a hole will swallow me. They then, out of pity, offer a selection of potential grooms, either their nephews from Lebanon or that one guy who's been married ten times with ten kids because what else should a girl expect when she reaches my age.

And if that's not bad enough, I now have to sit and listen to their high-school daughters whinge and whine about how they'll *die* if they reach my age with no ring, or how they're unable to fathom what I've been doing with my life for the past ten years. I could say that I have a double degree with a Masters in Teaching or that I've been offered a publishing contract for my first ever YA novel or that I was awarded a scholarship to complete my doctorate in Education, but again I nod and smile, waiting for the sun to set. Plus no-one likes to hear someone rant about their achievements like some kind of know-it-all.

'So, do you allow people to come and see her?' I hear one lady ask my mother like I'm some damsel in distress locked away in some dark tall tower. My brain has immediate flashbacks to the times I have accepted any potential offers to come over, which only makes my stomach turn. It's awkward, to say the least, especially with my family. My brothers along with my brothers-in-law and my uncle crowd into our small salon and basically flex their muscles and have a staring competition. It's not like they intentionally try to scare the bejesus out of the potential groom, but they each have a role to play. Conversations are short and stilted to begin with, before my brothers play their favourite game: 101 questions. They ask things like where he lives – not that they care about what suburb he's from, but depending on that suburb it could lead to knowing whether or not the groom associates with known criminals. They then ask about his job – i.e. that he's not in any drug-related gangs – and what gym he attends. If it's a mixed gym, then this potential groom is a waste of time because he could be a sleaze, and if it's an all-guys' gym, he could associate with shady people or drug dealers. Their questions never make any sense since we live in an area that makes the news for all the wrong reasons and my brothers attend the very gyms they despise and disapprove of. But I don't mind the questions because, like always, I can't seem to understand why I agreed to do this in the first place. And yes, I have a choice. I'm not forced into this pain.

Once the awkward chatter is out of the way, it's time to offer the potential groom and his family something to drink, which is done by my father. In my household a woman never serves in these types of social gatherings, rather she sits and relaxes; this reminds the groom that I am no waiter and that there'll be no chance to judge my *wifely* skills. I never like to make direct eye contact with my brothers because we have our own little games we play, with our own little codes to decide whether or not I should give any poor groom a chance. My brother's codes go as follows:

- Scrolling on the phone – find out more information, he could be worth it.
- Cracking fingers – don't even think about it.

- Scratch head – confused; he may be lying about what he said or things don't add up.
- Fake laugh – go outside to the kitchen so we can chat and debrief.
- Drink a full glass of drink – he's weird and the night needs to end.
- Blow nose loudly – abort mission now!

OK, I'm starting to see why I'm still single . . .

'So, I have a *3ariis*? He's very handsome,' the lady tries once more and I give my mother that look to change the subject, which my mother does, in her calm and collected manner.

The chatter and conversations continue without me and it's precisely this time when I take a couple of deep breaths and slowly drown out the noise. I enter my own little world where I don't have to answer people's ridiculous questions and prove that I have just as much to offer as any other woman. It's not the fact that I'm questioned about marriage that gives my social anxiety anxiety, it's the fact that I'm made to feel like I need rescuing or saving from a life that God hasn't planned for me yet.

It hits me – it's not Eid or the social events that I dread, it's the people. See, my type of anxiety is in the fine print. It's in people's stares and side comments, their never-ending list of expectations placed upon a girl they barely know, hidden beneath their 'good intentions'.

I miss the old me, the me who couldn't sleep at night because of how excited I was for the festivities of Eid, not because my bed was dressed fancier than me. I miss being of an age where I felt the excitement in the air not only because a month of fasting was complete but because my religion, the religion I love so much, began in a cave fifteen hundred years ago, called to a man, an extraordinary man with an incredible task. And then I hear my dad's voice: *Focus on something good.* It's in this moment where I glance over to see my nieces and nephews huddled around each other, giggling while comparing how much money they made and how many sweets they stuffed in their bags. I see the youngest of them all pull at her dad's trousers, trying to get his attention to open her third lollipop. I see my mum smile proudly as she fixes my brother's shirt while my sisters laugh at some video of a costume party their kids attended. I see my uncle playfully throw his daughter in the air like she is the only thing that matters, and then I turn to my dad, who doesn't say anything at all, just a gentle nod to let me know that it's OK and that he'll always be there for me, married or not.

Family. That's my anxiety's weakness.

The sun finally sets and the stars in the sky appear to signal my freedom. I stare into the bathroom mirror as the black ink mascara runs down my face and into the sink. My mask is washed away and I can finally see myself. I hang my clothes back into my cupboard and when I look up I notice the top shelf has been restocked with more pots and pans and kitchen utensils, otherwise known as *jhaz*, an Arab custom of buying things for a girl to prepare her for marriage. I quietly laugh to myself and try to ignore the reminder of being unmarried every time I open my cupboard. I can't help but feel bad for the numerous boxes that have collected dust still waiting for their new home.

My dad checks in and kisses me on my forehead before he reminds me of God's plan of greatness for me. I'm lucky that I have parents who raised me to chase my dreams and follow what my heart desired, no matter people's opinions. It's not to say that my mum doesn't want to see me in a white dress, I mean every mother would, but she knows things happen with good timing. Like the timing of this piece and how she couldn't help but smile at the idea that my name and face could reach a wider audience.

A wider, potential-filled Arab audience.

***Dr Paula Abood** has worked with diverse communities across Western Sydney for three decades and has written, directed and produced theatre and performance, literary publications and film over that time. In 2007, Paula completed a doctorate on race, gender and representation of Arabs in Australia. Paula received the Ros Bower Award in 2013 and an Australia Council Fellowship for Community Arts and Cultural Development in 2018.*

Once Upon a Time in the Diaspora

I write this on the lands of the traditional custodians, the Wallumattagal. I pay my heartfelt respects to the ancestors and elders, to the women whose backs have been broken by our presence here. I acknowledge sovereignty was never ceded; that we have soiled the lands and waters with our devastating footprint. For the suffering we have collectively caused to the First Peoples of the Land, I am eternally sorry.

Sitti J: أول الشجرة بذرة A tree begins with a seed.

I come from a long line of revolting women. A flush of rebellious naysaying types peppered my upbringing with audacious ideas about agency and autonomy. Some of the women were silent, even belligerent, randomly rising up, مِدَقّة in hand, making as much trouble as the moment might allow. Then there were those who agitated against any number of cross-sectarian patriarchs and colonial terrorists with a sense of militant fervour that got them effaced in perpetuity. Sure, some of the women in this narrative are whimsy; but others are altogether real and related.

The fictional ones traverse the ages, rampaging across the liminal spaces of my florid imaginary, sketching out various scenes; from a distant cousin forced to mask an ebullient sexuality to a great-aunt who hit her no-good husband over the head with a *tanjura*. In these parsed-up stories, at every turn, my sister-kin annihilate the brutish with a zeal that makes the post-colonial feminist squeal with delight were they to find such characters in a paper book of stories or digital web-series.

As for the real, all those who have mattered to me most in my becoming, have passed – الله يرحمها *Allah yerhama* – but left their mark on the second daughter of the second daughter. Tutored in the complex business of being by a divine mother, and blessed by the stories of the venerable grandmothers, I was washed in the rosewater of Arab diasporic feminist knowledge.

Sitti M: يا حياتي *ya hayati* العقل زينة The mind is decoration.

Growing up in Sydney in an established Maronite Lebanese family, I tended to the role of Dutiful Daughter like a fish in water. While this gendered personification is fluid and culturally specific depending on place, space and transience of time, the process of constructing self in my context is at once an intergenerational work in progress. I want to explore this idea of becoming as a gesture towards tracing out the cross-fertilisations of identity and history, unpacking the various parts of self that inform who and how we are in the world; how we become racialised, gendered, ethno-class inflected, sexual and spiritual subjects to a plenitude of peoples and publics. Indeed, in this transactional galaxy where the individuated self is idealised, an inquiry into selving becomes a mental imperative in order to stay dry in the ocean of self-delusion.

Arab-American anthropologist Suad Joseph argues in her reflection on gender, self and identity in Arab families that we are 'actively engaged in [our] own self-making'; that the 'self is always situated, contextualised, and embedded in relationships', and that 'selving is a lifelong process'.[1] Joseph's research speaks to my own thinking on models of selfhood that don't privilege the cult of the individual, but rather are multifaceted and relationally kinetic. My own trajectory of selving speaks precisely to this complexity, especially as the dynamics of family shift over time, and age and consciousness of agency deliver different kinds of

---

1 J. Berger, 'Ways of seeing', in A. Jones (ed.), *The Feminism and Visual Culture Reader*, 2nd edn, London and New York: Routledge, 2010, pp. 2–3.

conditions for, and of, being. In some ways, for me this is about accountability to a range of relational concerns via my ongoing engagement with a kind of feminist duty or *wajb*.

In reflecting on my feminist selving, it is the promise of my grandmothers that I recall; warrior women who yearned to write their names, to read poetry, letters and books, to be free of the shackles of drudgery. Women like my mother figure forcefully, wielding subversive power under the cover of domesticity, finding creative ways to express themselves in a world that devalues bold women who rock the patriarchal boat, rendering them adrift in the sea of forgetfulness.

Sitti M: يا حلوة y*a helweh* لا تأكل خبزك على مائدة غيرك Do not eat your bread on somebody else's table.

Indeed, my maternal grandmother's illiteracy was a driving force in my conscientisation. Sitti's frequent declamations about literacy meant that her daughters and granddaughters would not endure the social and political powerlessness of not being able to read and write. Signing her name was a struggle that I retain as a visual memory. Sitti made sure that her girls would have every possible opportunity to learn beyond what was socially expected of the female child; to rise up, emancipated as autonomous beings through the mode of institutional learning. This grandmother was not one to tolerate a whiff of male entitlement. If she ever came face to face with a bullish man, she would ply them with words soaked in centuries of mountain-grade vinegar, making a meal out of the grimmest of people.

Mama: الجهل شر الأصحاب Ignorance is the most terrible acquaintance.

My mother in turn cultivated a brilliant mind that sang to any child's sense of curious wonder. She, like her mother, was one to challenge the social status quo, especially if there was an injustice or inequality. Between her wise, deep-thinking father and socially astute mother, Mum was destined for a stellar career at a time when women were not encouraged to seek intellectual agency, or meaningful paid work outside the customary. Awarded a scholarship, Mum went to teacher's college in the 1950s and taught primary school children for several years before she married and produced her very own classroom of eight children. Then Mum's life changed radically as she became hermetically sealed in the domesticity of the unconventional.

To my mind, no-one has come close to my mother's capacity to nurture a pod of eight in all expressions of the intellectual, spiritual, moral and social. Together she and my much-loved father protected us from the toxic incursions both internally and externally. From the bloviating noise of white supremacy, to my father chasing cars up the street waving a pitchfork at the sheer disrespect of the wolf-whistler; to his father, my grandfather – the patriarch – threatening a violent man that, should he hit his wife again, there would be no mercy.

Sitti J: آفة العِلْم النسيان Forgetting is the plague of knowledge.

While the centrality of family underpins the heart of this essay, it is not my intention to idealise family, or community for that matter. Having worked in community for three decades, I am awake to the reality that family is indeed an oppressive site for many, namely those who endure violence in all its insidious forms, especially those whose non-binary, non-conforming gender and sexual identities and lives are viewed as 'transgressive' in the scheme of the hetero-normative.

Born into our clans and families, we are at once socialised into ethno-patriarchal systems of signs, behaviours, protocols, gendered roles and rules, all of which many of us expend the remainder of our psycho-socio-political lives attempting to unlearn, challenge, repudiate, disrupt and destroy. Whilst a plague of patriarchies have imposed their structures and systems on all of us from the village to the big city – and I emphatically mean to be inclusive of all here, be they gender-fluid, bi-gender, non-binary, non-conforming, transgender, questioning or genderqueer – I have never had a political dispute with being a dutiful daughter in and of itself, or for that matter with the idea of feminist *wajb*, most especially duty in the name of love, care and solidarity that works towards the dismantling of the hetero-patriarchal state.

Mama: الأيام دول Days are like countries.

Like my foremothers, it is the oppressive structures and violent technologies of masculinist power that afflict my sense of earthly justice and psychic peace. As I move through all the different spaces that constitute the private, intimate, public, community, social and not-so-social, I am reminded of John Berger's words in 'Ways of Seeing' that, 'a woman must continually watch herself . . . [w]hilst she is walking across a room or whilst she is weeping at the death of her father, she can scarcely avoid envisaging herself walking or weeping. From earliest childhood she has been taught and persuaded to survey herself continually'.[2] The hand of shame is always tugging at our female selves, making us vigilant to how we dress, how we look, how we cross our legs. Growing up in a household of women meant we made meaning out of these kinds of gendered tropes. Sharing knowledge kept us grounded and aware of how power works to contain and negate women and girls in every aspect of our lives.

The oppressive ways in which gender norms are imposed on us internally and externally inflects the selving process. Many in our communities are forced to endure homophobic and transphobic bullying and violence that goes unchecked across all faith groups. Though Joseph counsels, even patriarchy is 'not a fixed, stable social structure . . . but rather a historically changing, contextual, and subject to the power of specific personas,'[3] having to navigate racism, misogyny, homophobia, transphobia, and ableism is a harmful and painful reality that informs how we live our lives between the shadows and the light.

---

2 Berger, p. 42.

3 S. Joseph, 'Theories and dynamics of gender, self, and identity in Arab families', in S. Joseph (ed.), *Intimate Selving in Arab Families: Gender, Self, and Identity*, Syracuse: Syracuse University Press, 1999, p. 2.

Sitti J: إن مفاتيح الأمور العزائم Determination is the key to everything.

African-American feminist thinker bell hooks' childhood memories of talking back resonate with the kinds of power dynamics that underwrite our verbal responsiveness to living in a violent society. hooks writes, '"back talk" and "talking back" meant daring to disagree and sometimes it just meant having an opinion . . . To speak . . . when one was not spoken to was a courageous act – an act of risk and daring'.[4]

Considering all the environments in which we are socialised and conditioned as gendered, racialised sexualised subjects (and objects), I agree with hooks that speaking back is an act of great courage. It is not always possible. But when it is, it can inaugurate a process of breaking down the heft of power. And I know that is never easy; I know that for many women it is downright dangerous. For women who are stateless or seeking asylum, it can get you incarcerated or deported. For those in any kind of politically or socially precarious position, speaking back can get you abused, harmed or blacklisted.

I never take the material conditions of 'talking back' for granted. I also understand the sense of power that can be felt in 'coming to voice', because whilst women in my family possessed a certain agency, gender restrictions and

---

4 b. hooks, *Talking Back: Thinking Feminist, Thinking Black*, Boston: South End Press, 1989, p. 4.

racialised fear meant that we were raised *not* to speak up or back. It was seen as a sign of disrespect inside; to do so outside, a dangerous act in the white supremacist state. So for me, the struggle to speak back has always been about courage, responsibility, sensitivity and strategic intervention. As the saying goes, if you have an opinion, you better be determined. There have been many occasions I can recall where I have been wilfully excluded or banned because I have been pegged as a troublemaker, just like my mother and grandmothers before me. When excluded, I use the anger that inevitably comes with, to create alternative spaces to express. I have especially used art and culture like my grandmother as a tool to speak on my own terms and thus return to my own source of power.

Sitti M: مفيش حلاوة من غير نار There is no sweetness without fire.

My sense of feminist *wajb* has grown to be expansive, linking the emotional memory of my grandmothers to my everyday work with migrant and refugee women whose struggles resonate across an intergenerational consciousness. The idea of the dutiful daughter has come to mean something beyond the familial relation, namely in the struggle for social justice, especially in the work of solidarity with the vulnerable, those seeking asylum, women escaping violence. This is where *wajb*, as a social and political responsibility, is present and meaningful for me as an activist, advocate and community worker.

For the conscientious dutiful daughter, self-care is thus crucial. As affective beings, we must learn to breathe. It is here my grandmother Jawhara guides me to the light. Watching her crochet a landscape of textures was like watching her pray. A deeply meditative art form, crochet provided my grandmother with a creative conduit in her life as a woman of family, faith and community. Her crochet hook and fine cotton thread were her prayer beads as she counted out the geometrics of imagery into quiet works of devotional art.

Sitti developed a strategy to survive in the monolingual state, a state that double-disses her mother tongue into the present. Language remains a contested terrain and Sitti stood her linguistic ground. In the midst of white supremacy, she refused to speak English. She dedicated herself to other ways of being in the multicultural state. She taught us that integrating into the dead weight of the dominant culture meant growing up mediocre. And who would choose that? She recycled everything and wasted nothing. She was she keeper of plant-based-healing knowledge that was passed on to my father and in turn her grandchildren. I have taken up all my grandmother's ways as my selving moves to the next stage.

Aunty J: إن مع اليوم غدا يا مسعدة There's always tomorrow.

My morning coffee cup counsels insolence. The kind that gets you into trouble. In this coffee cup vignette, the wayward woman is not so much a burden as a life choice. It speaks to a grandmother's whisper in our diasporic ear.

No crowd ever waited at the gates of patience. *Sabr* is what you need to make coffee, not to fight the five faces of oppression.[5]

As a child, we were socialised to wonder why *that* aunt didn't get married, only because the adults around us referred to *that* aunt as 'the one who didn't get married'. It seemed to be a kind of stigma, because it was whispered about, and yet here I am, the aunt who didn't get married. Blessed be my nieces and nephews who are mighty thankful for that.

To that end, my aim يا روحي *ya rouhi* is to parse a different kind of duty; one part dissident, one part difficult, there is no time to waste. And so, the dutiful daughter seamlessly transforms into the Dutiful Aunt. Perhaps this is the most nourishing kind of selving there is in this world.

5 I.M. Young, 'Five faces of oppression', in J. DeFilippis & S. Saegert (eds), *The Community Development Reader*, 2008, p. 276.

***Ryan Al-Natour** has lived all over Western Sydney (Dharug Country), Rockhampton (Dharrumbal Country) and Dubbo (Wiradjuri Country). He completed his honours degree in Social Sciences at the University of New South Wales and his Doctorate at Western Sydney University. He currently works as a lecturer at Charles Sturt University and enjoys reading about Indigenous and anti-racist pedagogies, boxing, cooking, gardening, movies, kayaking and learning Auslan.*

Racism and Recipes

I had just arrived to officially begin a new life for myself in the Sunshine State. I'd spent the previous week driving up from Western Sydney. I was born in Canterbury to Palestinian parents and I'd lived in Blacktown, Parramatta, Mount Druitt and Bankstown for most of my life. I had also spent two years in Palestine as a teenager. For me, Queensland was a holiday destination filled with theme parks, beaches, hot weather, wildlife and fresh tropical fruits. I remember when my late father took me on holidays to Bundaberg, the Gold Coast and Brisbane when I was eleven, before he passed. Now, as an adult, I had accepted a job offer and made the decision to move to regional Queensland. This was my opportunity to live in a warmer climate where

I could swim all year round, avoid overpriced Sydney rent and the congestion of an increasingly densely populated urban jungle. In my new life in Queensland, I could rent a two-bedroom house with a giant backyard for even less than the cost of a small room in a shared Sydney apartment.

Bring. It. On. I thought.

Surprisingly, it was difficult to find a property to rent in Rockhampton before moving. When I initially phoned as Ryan Al-Natour, a real estate agent told me 'we don't want too many people living here'. Ryan Smith phoned back and made an appointment to inspect the property. On one occasion I inspected a house as the landlords next door watched me curiously. When I applied for this house, these landlords suddenly increased the rent by twenty dollars a week. On another occasion, a real estate agent commented that I should be careful renting in Rockhampton as there were 'feral Indigenous' people around. I withdrew my application.

Rockhampton is known as the beef capital of Australia. After passing the 'Welcome to Rockhampton' sign and numerous giant statues of bulls and cows, I noticed that it was 2 pm. I had missed lunch. I googled 'best steak in Rockhampton' and ended up at a random pub. It was after the lunchtime rush and I was the only person in the entire pub. The steak was served on a sizzling hot plate and it was delicious.

The waitress asked about my meal. There was something about her. I wasn't sure whether she was angry, annoyed or nervous. I could sense a strange vibe that prompted me to be extra friendly, thanking her a few times for a great meal. She told me information about the high-quality, grass-fed beef I had eaten. We started chatting about other items on the menu like kangaroo, crocodile and emu. I wasn't used to seeing these items on a Western Sydney menu. She then paused, looked away and told me that they kept halal meat in the kitchen. This information came out of nowhere. Her voice tone went from being 'informative' about the menu to being 'annoyed'.

She must think I am Muslim, I thought. I informed her that if eating halal meat were a priority for me, I would have asked about it before finishing an entire steak.

The waitress then shared her thoughts.

'We shouldn't have to keep halal meat.

'We shouldn't have to change the menu.

'We shouldn't cater for that!'

It struck me then. She wasn't opening up a can of halal worms with the intention of being educated about Muslims and protocol. The waitress wanted an argument.

I started to become annoyed.

'Then don't keep halal meat.

'Then don't change the menu.

'It is not my restaurant, I don't care what you serve.'

I had only been in Rockhampton for two hours. Was it arduous to be Arab-Australian in Rockhampton? Was racism a common day-to-day experience?

My father's side of the family is fair-skinned. When my Father and *amo* (uncle) sailed to Australia during the white Australia policy era, people often read their appearance as European. I am dark-skinned and proudly 'of Middle Eastern appearance' – despite the media/policing abuse of this as a racialised descriptor. Unlike my uncles and some of my cousins, no-one would mistakenly think I am white.

The waitress didn't do anything unusual in assuming that I was Muslim. Perhaps it is common for non-Arabs to assume that all Arabs are Muslim – even though the majority of Arab-Australians are Christians. I don't have a problem with being mistaken as Muslim. A sizable portion of Palestinians are Orthodox Christians and we are proudly a culturally Islamic society. In Western Sydney the diversity within Arab communities is commonly overlooked and I grew up challenging a common assumption that all Arabs are 'Lebs'. Further, in the ignorant minds of some Islamophobes, the term 'Muslim' is often conflated with the identities of 'Arab', 'Lebanese', and 'Middle Eastern'. From the 1990s onwards, a series of dominant discourses have linked these identities to a series of derogatory anti-Arab male stereotypes. Hollywood/tabloid news screens fetishise Arab men in many ways, ranging from the ultra-masculine misogynist leading a harem, to the indoctrinated terrorist. The first time I was called a terrorist was in the week after the events of September 11. I was nineteen and walking to Penrith train station when two men claimed that I had a bomb in my violin case. No-one dared call me a terrorist to my face until 2014 when a former student at a university I worked at put in a complaint about me. In this complaint, the student alleged that I had told students I intended to leave Australia and fight for ISIS. A supervisor, upon hearing this complaint had been made, asked me, 'I just need to know – is there anything true about it?'

I stared at him. Stayed silent for a good ten seconds. Was this actually happening?

'No,' I said.

Back to Rockhampton, where it had taken two hours for me – a Palestinian-Arab-Christian – to experience some form of Islamophobia in my new home. Surely this was a one-off incident? I was just unlucky? Right?

Wrong.

The next day a white man delivering my new fridge informed me that he knew I was a 'wog' from my last name on the customer receipt. The day after, a white woman told me (yes, again – out of nowhere) that Australia was under threat from Middle Eastern men who were secretly working for ISIS. A week later when I went to enquire about setting up an internet connection, a white woman told me she had been to Turkey where a lot of people looked like me. Pauline Hanson would frequently visit Rockhampton and I tweeted that bigotry would re-elect her into the senate. On social media her supporters trolled me with accusations that I was an ISIS-sympathiser, a 'sand man', and one person even sent me a picture of a gun. Within my new workplace, things were not easier. Behind my back, colleagues identified me as 'someone from overseas'. One colleague told me that her husband was 'like me' because he was an Indonesian. In passing, another person described me as a 'really good-looking Indian'. When I attended a writers' retreat, I was placed into a group with three white females. Our first activity was to identify a name for our group. One woman stared at me and said, 'We are very multicultural!'

Perhaps one of the most memorable instances was when a random white male talked about me – in front of me – to his friends as they walked past.

'Look at Raul over there!' he yelled as if this was an insult.

Something within me snapped. I responded with rage.

'MY NAME IS NOT RAUL!'

He looked scared. The crazy angry Arab male that he probably saw depicted on *A Current Affair* had just paid him a visit.

'Oh sorry, I thought it was.'

'You think every person with a tan has the same name?'

He ran away. His friends followed him.

Stereotype confirmed.

I wasn't the first Arab to set foot in Rockhampton. Anne Mansour is a Brisbane historian who has documented the presence of Lebanese across Queensland since the 1800s. Notably one of the most racist and homophobic politicians from north Queensland, the cowboy-hat-wearing Bob Katter, has Lebanese ancestry. Whenever journalists have asked Katter about his ancestry, he has always reacted in a hostile manner. In one instance he accused a reporter of being 'racist' because she asked about his 'Lebanese' grandfather. Another time Katter was interviewed on Sky News and an interviewer asked him about his Lebanese ancestry. Katter's smile quickly disappeared and he spoke of how rude it was to ask someone about their ancestry. Katter has repeatedly called for a moratorium on immigration from the Middle

East and North Africa. He made me wonder if this was what it took to survive and thrive in Queensland – deny your heritage to the point where you need to publicly hate on your own mob. Would I need to replace my keffiyeh with a cowboy hat?

That wouldn't be happening.

I spent Easter with a Lebanese family whose grandparents moved to Rocky in the 1850s. They did not speak a word of Arabic. They did not identify with their religion of origin (in their case it was Maronite). I spoke with various family members at this gathering and asked what it was like to be Arab in Rockhampton. I discovered that there was a sparse, scattered community. Interestingly, one component of Arab culture that had managed to survive the assimilation and white Australia policy eras in Queensland was the cuisine. At this particular gathering I was stoked that there was Arabic food! There was *malfoof* (cabbage rolls stuffed with rice and meat), *imjadereh* (brown lentils, onions and rice) and rice pudding.

A popular Arabic dish *kibbeh* (minced lamb or beef with bulghur, onion, spices and pine nuts) has two popular variations in Palestine. These include *kibbeh bil saniyeh* (served in a tray) and fried *kibbeh* (shaped like NRL-balls with mince and pine nuts in the centre – or what my *khalto*'s (auntie's) German husband calls 'footballs'). Growing up in Western Sydney, I noticed that the Lebanese had another variation: *kibbeh nayeh* (a raw version of the aforementioned recipes). This variation makes my stomach turn. It was served at this particular Easter gathering in Rockhampton. Of all aspects of Lebanese culture that survived in a racist Queensland climate – *kibbeh nayeh* of all things!

A friend at this gathering gave me a few vegetables I had trouble finding in Rockhampton: a bag of okra and a few zucchinis. Okra isn't a popular vegetable in regional Australia. As for zucchini – yes, you can purchase green zucchini in any supermarket. I discovered that what I had called 'zucchini' growing up is in fact called 'Lebanese zucchini' in Australia. I remember being at a local produce shop in Bundaberg and I asked a shopkeeper where I could find a different type of zucchini, showing her a picture of it on my iPhone.

'Oh, Lebanese zucchini,' she said. She mentioned that a local Turkish and Lebanese community grew it. I later found 'Lebanese zucchini' seeds.

As Palestinians in Australia, we frequently use 'Lebanese zucchini' in making *mahshi* (zucchini stuffed with rice, meat and herbs cooked in a tomato stew). I wonder if Australians might start calling it 'Palestinian zucchini' too.

Then again, if we do, I have a feeling that the state of Israel would appropriate it as Israeli cuisine and bastardise it.

I will not say that all my interactions with people in Rockhampton were based on racism. I admired progressive local residents who had grown up in conservative, regional Queensland and were active on social justice issues. A local conservative politician created a big sign in the middle of town reading 'Stop the Boats'. It was graffitied and changed to 'Stop the Goats'. At the time of Pauline Hanson's re-entrance into parliament after a twenty-year sabbatical, progressive residents frequently clashed with her local supporters. Whenever there was anything about Arabs or Muslims sensationalised on the news, a work colleague would check in with me. On one occasion he told me that if I did experience any racism in Rockhampton he would be sorry and wanted me to know that he had my back.

This colleague was an Aboriginal man and a gardening guru. He had a huge garden with a variety of herbs and vegetables. I used to get lost exploring his garden. He had a sophisticated system of creating compost and growing fresh produce. He even helped me grow Lebanese/Palestinian zucchini. Interestingly, he enabled me to culturally connect to Arab cuisine in ways that I had not growing up in Western Sydney. The taste of the herbs and vegies that grew in his garden reminded me of the tastes of vegetables I had eaten in Palestine. It was an unexpected nostalgic outcome of moving to regional Queensland.

Unlike Western Sydney, Rockhampton does not have a smorgasbord of Arabic restaurants selling hummus, felafel and tabouli (unlike the previously mentioned dishes, I have a feeling that I might not need to explain these to readers). If, say, I wanted a plate of tabouli in Bankstown, I could easily buy it from any number of restaurants. If, say, I wanted *manoush bi za'atar* (thyme/sumac/marjoram/olive oil/ with sesame seeds 'pizza'), I could go to any number of Arabic bakeries. If, say, I wanted to buy *labneh* (drained yoghurt with salt and olive oil), I could go to one of many Arab grocers. If, say, I wanted to buy *kifta* (minced lamb or beef mixed with herbs, onion and parsley), I could buy it mixed and prepared from any Arab butcher. The convenience is all over Western Sydney and I realised that I had taken it for granted.

Living in regional Australia means that you are deprived of this convenient access to your own mob's cuisine. There was no Arab bakery, butcher, grocer or restaurant in Rockhampton – and no, I will not recognise the doner kebab shops that offered pineapple as a filling. In regional Australia you need to find someone who grows your produce or grow it yourself. It means that your lazy ass needs to take the initiative and make your ancestral food from scratch. With the advantage of fresh produce on my side, my life in Rockhampton encouraged me to have several Arab 'aha' moments. For the first time in my life I made *labneh* using a cheesecloth (I didn't even know what a cheesecloth was!). I mixed my own herbs to make *za'atar*. I mastered *loubiyeh bil zeit* (green beans with tomato, onion and garlic) after my first attempt. I even made *kibbeh bil saniyeh* with the help of a ninety-year-old *amto* (auntie) who Skyped with me from Chicago, inspected the bulghur through her phone and asked when I was going to get married and start giving her grandnieces/nephews. My *amto* had a typical Arab ability of passing on recipes with a side of guilt. One time a white friend saw me talking to *Amto* on my phone and asked whether my aunt dyed her hair. Could it not be possible that the matriarch of my family was a blue-eyed, red-haired fair-skinned Palestinian woman? Non-Arabs have a habit of reminding me that I apparently look 'more Arab' than my family.

I called my *amo* in Mount Druitt – the one who notoriously makes the best hummus.

'*Amo,*' I pleaded. 'I have been trying to make my hummus really smooth. What's your secret?'

'When you come visit, I'll show you.'

Darn it. In desperation I bought hummus from a supermarket. It had *khal* (vinegar) in it. I threw it out.

A year after moving to Rockhamptom I visited Sydney. It alarmed me to realise how much I had changed as a person. I found the traffic unbearable. Giant buildings had appeared in my old stomping grounds. I loved showing all my old friends pictures of the kangaroos around my home, the two giant emus that chased me, the geckoes that lived in my kitchen, the possum that ate all my parsley, and giant crocodiles! I went to Mount Druitt and saw my *amo*. I had waited a whole year for the perfect hummus recipe he had promised to share. I turned up, eager to watch and learn.

My *amo* didn't *show* me how to make hummus as I'd expected. He *told* me his secret ingredient and the significance of blending certain ingredients in a particular order.

When I flew back home, I thought to myself: why couldn't he have told me this over the phone? Why did he have to wait until I visited him?

Then it clicked.

My *amo* didn't want to share this over a quick phone chat. Rather, he wanted to see how his nephew was doing up north. Arab cuisine is traditionally passed down from one generation by watching and learning. Recipes can be part of storytelling conversations – about life in the motherland, exploring Australia with my father, politics in Palestine, discussions about current affairs, how certain ingredients help you focus, and how certain foods are eaten at certain times of the year. This is all served with reminders that I apparently need to settle down soon as the matriarch, my *amto*, has probably already picked out the names of my children. A recipe is history. It's ancestry. It's culture. It's language. It's family. It's about surviving in the diaspora on Aboriginal land as Arab Australia.

I get it now.

By the way, no, I will not be sharing the secret ingredient for the perfect hummus.

***Amani Haydar** is an artist, lawyer, mum and advocate for women's health and safety based in Western Sydney. Amani's writing and illustrations have been published in* ABC News Online *and* SBS Life *and her self-portrait* Insert Headline Here *was a finalist in the 2018 Archibald Prize. Amani uses visual art and writing to explore the personal and political dimensions of abuse, loss, identity and resilience.*

The Pleasure and Privilege of Painting Flowers

In kindergarten I drew a crayon picture of a garden. Standing tall in the garden were two large flowers. The flowers had faces and they were smiling. With them stood a smiling girl with a mass of curly hair and three stick fingers at the end of each stick arm. In the waxy-blue-scribble sky above, the sun was smiling too.

My teacher, Mrs Di Bello, loved it so much she had it laminated and hung in the classroom.

It would be many years before I would put together my first art exhibition or have my work hung in a gallery, but it was just as special. Mrs Di Bello told Mum about my work.

Through soft brown eyes and a proud rosy smile, Mum approved. Addicted, I spent school holidays filling exercise books with illustrations and marvelling over the range of shades in my set of pencils: terracotta, vermillion, periwinkle.

I asked my mum to buy me supplies instead of toys for birthdays and she did, on the condition that it would not distract me from my studies. Proud but traditional, my parents were careful to rein in my creativity. 'Art is not a career, do not forget about your homework,' they warned.

Dad didn't think art was a serious thing. He liked talking about school and history, lamenting the war in Lebanon and the Israeli occupation in the south and sharing stories of his childhood. He liked conservative people who had degrees and titles. Dad wasn't a man of leisure.

'Aim for the moon and if you miss you'll land among the stars,' he would say.

Dad was a taxi driver but had two masters degrees in linguistics, which he had earned as a mature-aged student. He was qualified to interpret English into Arabic and made it a hobby to memorise English idioms and Aussie colloquialisms. We joked that he read dictionaries for fun. He buried his square face behind square books and looked up occasionally through big square glasses. He was quite formal and detached with me, but I thought he was very clever.

'You should be a doctor or a teacher,' Dad proposed. 'They are good jobs for a woman with a family.'

A woman with a family. Was that the moon or the stars?

I was hardly a woman and hadn't even thought about

having a family. However, I knew that when the time came to make serious decisions about my future I would have to choose from a set of options that would please my parents. It would have to be something suitable for a girl; something which did not involve travel, late nights or being outspoken. A job that would take up just enough of me so that enough was left over for everybody else.

So-and-so's daughter got a UAI of ninety-something-point-something (we call it an ATAR now) and became a doctor. I needed to be as good, or better.

First, I needed to get into my local girls' selective high school. That was the moon.

At St George Girls' High the uniforms were old-fashioned, and the front entrance was grander than those of the other schools in the local area. There were jolly rose-bushes along the fence and mighty sycamores either side of an austere brick porch. I wanted to get in so badly, albeit for different reasons than my parents – I wanted the validation. After a few weeks of intensive tutoring at a coaching centre in Belmore, where I was the only curly-haired Arab girl in a class of gifted students from Chinese and Korean backgrounds, that goal started to feel unrealistic. I got about four out of twenty for every maths quiz, six weeks straight. I can still see those marks scrawled on the page in offensive red ink.

Many years later, when I decided to get married, Dad bragged about what a wonderful daughter he had brought up. 'I've never raised a hand at her!' he told my in-laws proudly when they came to ask for my hand over tea and *baklawa* in my parents' backyard. I agreed with a shy smile and let myself feel proud until I wasn't sure who was the bigger imposter.

As I stared at the struggling *zaytoon* tree in the back corner, I remembered preparing for selective school entry exams. I remembered Dad teaching me to convert fractions into percentages after another four out of twenty. I became frustrated at myself as I struggled to wrap my head around the concept. I hated myself for not knowing. I felt embarrassed that I didn't know the answer and guilty that my parents were spending so much money and time on coaching.

When a sob escaped Dad shouted, 'WHY ARE YOU CRYING?'

Ashamed but no longer in control of my emotions, I cried harder. My anxious mind painted a scene: I would miss out on the selective school, fail year 12 and end up homeless under a bridge somewhere. On drugs, with a torn shirt and holes in my shoes!

Before I could calm myself, I felt the force of Dad's palm across my face. When he pulled his hand away, my cheek felt hot and tingly from the blast. My nose pulsed and began to bleed. I didn't know where to look. The lesson was over. Blood and tears dropped onto the page of my exercise book.

So, the truth is, Dad almost never hit me. He *rarely* raised a hand. But I rarely failed, made mistakes or cried; at least not around him.

*

Four out of twenty is twenty percent. With a mark like that I couldn't impress the coaching centre, and I couldn't impress my family. There must be more to life than maths though, because I got into St George Girls' and studied on jacaranda carpets in its sunny quadrangles.

At home my parents fought endlessly and repeatedly to the brink of divorce. At school, with friends, I was busy and happy, but I wasn't allowed to socialise on weekends or holidays. I did not always have the energy to fight and beg to go to the movies or a friend's place. My friends did not share my Arab heritage and did not understand my parents' anxieties, so they gave me silly advice like 'this is your life' and 'you should threaten to run away'.

Art was my favourite subject but at home art-making went underground. While other year 9 girls hid cigarettes and boyfriends, I hid my creativity. I studied all afternoon so I could work on my art unmonitored and unjudged in the night. Sometimes I even stayed up after *fajr* prayers to work on my visual arts projects or decorate my school-issued homework diary. Instead of tasks and deadlines I filled the diary with bubble writing and rap songs. Some pages were filled with hand-lettered Eminem lyrics, and others were a montage of magazine cut-outs, photos of friends and glued-in high school ephemera. I scrapbooked notes passed around in class and invitations to parties I was not allowed to attend.

'This is *vandalism*,' my year 9 science teacher said when she confiscated the diary because schoolmates marvelling over its rainbow pages had disrupted her class.

That year I received a bad maths report.

Amani needs to be more active in her efforts to understand the content of this subject by completing her homework on time and revising work frequently. She needs to concentrate on her work in class and make a more consistent effort.

It was the end of the world as far as Dad was concerned. He went to see my maths teacher on parent-teacher interview night. Anxious about what would be exchanged between the two men, I decided to strategically tag along. *If I'm there he might feel pressured to say something nice*, I thought.

'Amani talks too much,' my teacher said, looking down at a piece of paper.

Shit.

Dad was respectable back then, so he hung his head in profound shame. His jowls sagged and his eyes ran from mine. He was sorry that he had had anything to do with my abysmal algebra.

Fifteen years later, when Dad went to trial for murder, I walked into the courtroom and searched his face for that shame. I wanted so terribly to find a way not to hate him. I wanted a reason to let go of some of the anger. For twenty-six years I had refined the art of seeking his approval and detecting his disappointment. I looked for shame as the judge pronounced him guilty. Instead, as court officers came to cuff him, Dad puffed his chest and held his head high. He even waved and thanked his family for being there.

On parent-teacher night, however, Dad rushed out of the school hall with his head still hanging while I desperately tried to redeem myself. I gestured towards my artworks which were on display in the foyer. 'That's my painting!' His jaw was clenched and he did not look up.

After that interview Dad said he was disappointed and that all his hard work and sacrifice was so that I would be successful. He said he never planned to be in Australia forever but had stayed for the opportunities it gave his children and his entire life here would be a waste if we failed. I felt sorry for him; he did not have the moon or the stars and that was somehow my fault.

The next day, with all the melodrama of fourteen-going-on-fifteen, I wrote:

> *. . . as I sit here at my desk, hearing Dad's yelling, angry voice . . . my life has shrivelled into a puddle of incompetence, insecurity, sadness, pressure, frustration and despair . . . Last night was parent-teacher night; probably the worst thing that could've happened to me! My teacher said I talk too much . . . My parents now think that we are failures and they are thinking of moving back to Lebanon. They reckon they are only here for our education and we 'don't care' about our education so they have an excuse to go back . . . I don't want to move to Lebanon.*

It was a miserable and lonely time and I was too young to understand that my parents were trying to remedy their losses and anxieties through me. I did not realise they were grieving a homeland they had started to realise they might never see again, even though the occupation had ended and others had returned. Maybe they knew we could never move back and needed to feel that life in the *ghurbi* was worthwhile.

We stayed here. I disciplined my mind and self-soothed with positive mantras: *fake it till you make it.* I redeemed myself at the end of that year with a better report in which one teacher wrote, *Amani is a cheerful student.*

I read something recently about parental expectations in migrant families. Researchers say high parental expectation plays a 'critical role in children's academic success'. Children whose parents expect them to do well academically are more likely to receive higher grades and even stay in school longer. Our migrant parents wanted us to experience security and social mobility. Maybe they could not have that themselves; their skills and education did not translate here, and they landed in low-paying factory jobs or got stuck driving a taxi. Maybe they felt overwhelmed and afraid of change. They fled villages and expected us to build cities with their sacrifices.

As expected, throughout my senior years I became very good at maths. When I got my ninety-something-point-something, cousins and relatives brought sweets and said kind things that made me feel like I could do anything. Mum bought me a pair of gold earrings. I went to university and studied law and communications, having decided that I wanted to understand people, help them tell their stories and get their justice.

Maybe high expectations got me to the moon. But where do we draw the line between expectation and abuse? When I have confidential conversations with women whose parents did not let them read fiction or draw, they tell me their stories with a profound sense of loss. They do not say, '*Alhamdulillah*, I learned long division instead!' They yearn for the joy and individuality they felt when they were making inimitable marks with crayons and pencils. They tell me their father hit them a few times, and their mum feared him, but they would not dare speak openly about that.

I keep their secrets, but I do them justice by sharing mine.

We know that our parents made sacrifices. We know that they compromised their moons, believing they were sending us to the stars. But in their desperation to recover from homeland wars and see us rebuild what they had lost, they conscripted us to battles that had already stopped making sense.

As a commercial lawyer I spent years tethered to a desk in a grey office on level 31. I didn't hate it, but I didn't love it either. The hours were long and lonely, and my mind needed to be focused and disciplined. Even all those floors up above Sydney, the creative itch lingered. To relieve anxiety, I would take the elevator and wander down to a nearby bookstore to browse the art section. I escaped into the golds of Klimt, the blues of Chagall, the reds of Matisse. I fawned over the magic in the works of Del Kathryn Barton; her waratahs and marsupials made me feel both foreign and at home. Then I would drag myself away, back up the elevator into my glass cell where the air smelled like warm paper and computer parts.

It is very impolite in Arab culture to speak poorly of your parents. In Muslim families we are taught that our parents are keys to the gates of *Jannah*. I have met people who misunderstand that to mean that we should accept everything our parents do, no matter what they have done to us. I have heard people use those teachings to justify abuse, to explain why they live a shadow life of unmet ambitions. I was standing in Queen's Square with my baby in his pram after having read my victim impact statement at my father's trial, when an uncle yelled, 'You wouldn't even be a lawyer if it weren't for him!' Cousins who knew nothing about me accused me of disobedience and disloyalty.

I am many things and none of them belong to my father. The battles I'd fought to make him proud stopped making sense when he murdered my mum. After the trial I resigned from my job, for myself and for my family. I needed to paint and spend time re-imagining my life. As I painted I healed, and as I healed inspiration came frothing to the surface. For every hour I spent painting, at first, I counted the billable units I'd lost. I felt guilty that I was wasting my time on something that was not difficult or painful. I read articles that told me social conditioning and fanatical capitalism make women who choose creative careers feel this way. Art can't be time-costed and measured. It has an intangible quality that doesn't easily translate into money sums or mathematical formulae.

I gave myself permission to do it anyway and when the evening news called my work 'defiant', I pictured my father sitting in his cell, watching. Since then I have been giving myself permission to make art professionally and it has been liberating. Still, I worry that by leaving one mould I am being poured to set in another. I admire artists who make art for art's sake and I think of how long I have waited for the freedom to create. Yet I struggle with guilt when I paint a still life or *just* flowers. What does it mean to paint a teapot or a pot plant when the world is falling apart around you?

Am I entitled to the pleasure and privilege of painting flowers? Can I paint golden banksias and intense cobalt skies if I am also painting banners that shout, 'Stop violence against women!' and documenting three generations of pain? If I write or paint about something other than abuse or hyphenated identities, will it still be art?

I answer those questions for myself: everything is political, even painting flowers. Every mark or gesture is a rebellion against parental expectation, control and unforgiving violence. By giving myself permission to indulge, to break away from the full-time jobs of breaking stereotypes and revisiting garish memories to teach unteachable things, I give myself permission to exist outside of what is meant to define me.

Sometimes I just want to paint flowers.

There is a power in painting both the light and the dark in life, the traumatic and the trivial. It says: we are here, our stories are real. We deserve to have them heard.

The little girl who drew flowers with faces and a smiling sun deserves that too.

Miran Hosny is a Sydney lawyer with a background in journalism. She was co-editor of Arab-Australian publication Sajjeling, *radio producer at the ABC, and produced current affairs program* The Y Factor *for community radio. She currently dabbles in comic illustration, with varying degrees of (non)success.*

Blue-label Memoirs

It is a truth universally acknowledged, affirmed, broadcasted, reiterated and shouted in caps lock from the interface of every relevant blog that Arabs are not one homogenous group of people.

But I'm not here to correct fake news.

My story begins with a startling epiphany realised as I gazed at my distorted reflection in the dull brassy interior of an emptied hommus dip can (the authentic, blue-label Cortas hommus of course, not the knock-off white-bread supermarket concoction).

Not being one to accept inspiration unquestioningly – hold that against me if you will, but overthinking and dissecting overthought thoughts is my forte – I pulled my gaze from the hommus can and tapped out a question to my cousins in Egypt.

What speaks 'childhood' to you?

And the answers came.

Silver triangle juice poppers from a brand called Best.

Taking crates of empty glass Pepsi bottles to the corner shop and swapping them for coins or more Pepsi.

Watching Bakkar, *a cartoon about a Nubian Egyptian boy's adventures in Aswan with his goat.*

Playing a game called 'el-nahla'. Ask your dad about it.

Playing hide and seek in the gardens and bedrooms at our great-grandfather's estate – ask your mum about it.

Summers at the old beach chalets in Maamoura.

Playing soccer in the neighbourhood laneways.

Buying freska from the wandering vendor on the beach in summer.

Hearing the cannon boom for iftaar time in Ramadan.

The rubabekya guy yelling 'bekyaaa' as he pulled his donkey and cart down the neighbourhood streets to let us know he was buying and selling pre-loved items. He made vintage mobile before 'vintage' was even in.

Visiting Grandfather's grave after Friday prayers.

Raising ducks on our apartment building rooftop when our mum and aunt were going through an 'organic' phase.

Buying every new edition of the 'Mickey' magazine from the newsagent stand at the tram station in Old Alexandria back when it was downtown and not 'old town' to us.

Amr Diab's many hair phases.

Though the list is by no means exhaustive, it moved the dial on my epiphany from 'hypothesis' to 'valid theory'.

You see, I simply cannot relate.

I am often asked about my ethno-cultural heritage, and depending on how the question is posed I usually offer an answer along the lines that my parents originally hail from Egypt.

The reactions to that are as varied as they are predictable.

'Oh cool! Are you related to Tamer Hosny then?' (No.)

'Wow! Egypt! Those pyramids are really something, hey?' (I suppose you could call them a wonder.)

'Can you speak Hieroglyphic?' (I have no words.)

'You must be amazing at bellydancing. Show us some moves!' (Scientists have yet to discover the hereditary gene pattern for dance.)

'Egyptian *molokheya* is weird and soupy. I don't like it. Our *molokheya* is better.' (Insult *molokheya* at your own risk. Battle lines will be drawn.)

'Ohhh so that's why you're darker. And your eyes! So Cleopatra!' (Not your exotic.)

'You're Egyptian?! *IZZAYEK! HAGA HAGA! KWAYES!*' (Believe it or not, this isn't the national motto.)

As much as I love Egyptian culture – which, to be clear, is made up of so much more than pharaohs, bellydancers and Tamer Hosnys – my personal strain of ethnic culture cannot truthfully be described as purely Egyptian.

My childhood memories of Ramadan are of Mama sending me on walks to a Lebanese shop in Punchbowl to buy *mayy zahr* and *atayef* in Ramadan, and then swapping our Palestinian family friends a plate of Egyptian *atayef* stuffed with mixed nuts and raisins for a plate of Gazan-style sweet-cheese *atayef*.

On Eid-ul-Fitr we broke our fasts on *manoush* then swapped trays of *kahk* for our Lebanese family friends' *maamoul* and our Iraqi friends' *klechas*. We lined up for stretchy Syrian milk ice cream at the annual Syrian merchants' expo, and I wised up enough to realise that it is always necessary to check which *fasolya* or *lubya* is under discussion in any food conversation between Levantines and non-Levantines.

We ate our couscous with meatballs, and we sometimes popped noodles into our lentil soup. We grew mint and basil in our backyard for tea, and learned to sniff water bottles before drinking from them if Teta was in town – she has a thing for mixing rosewater into drinking water for the 'scent'.

Where my cousins lined up at their local *fool* store in Egypt to buy breakfasts of multi-flavoured *fool* and falafel – chilli stuffed, lemony, olive oiled, tahini mixed, pastrami stuffed – my siblings and I ate cereal on weekdays and pulled out Mama's *'edra* from the old country to stew fava beans overnight for preparing *fool* from scratch for the weekends. We made Egyptian falafel mix in bulk for freezing because there were no Egyptian restaurants that we knew of from which we could purchase the traditional fare, and on our lazy days we pulled out California fava bean cans and bought Lebanese falafel from Jasmines.

No family barbecue or picnic was complete without tabbouleh, fattoush and hommus. No celebration was quite as festive as when our Algerian friends brought out trays of shiny almond-meal desserts shaped like the most succulent of fruits. No visit was as cleansing – though potentially asthma-attack inducing – as those spent sitting under plumes of incense smoke at Palestinian and Khaleeji friends' homes.

Summer, to me, was inflatable pools in our backyard in Hinchinbrook, watching a bird's eggs hatch in the nest it laid on our rotary clothes line in Greenacre, playing cricket with my siblings at our neighbourhood parks, holidaying in Nelson Bay, taking long ice-cream filled walks on the beaches of Brighton-le-Sands – which my parents loved for how it reminded them of the corniche of the Greco-Roman Egyptian city of Alexandria – riding bikes everywhere, getting stung by a jellyfish at Carss Park, making ice blocks at home under the chirpy monitoring of colourful lorikeets who hung in the trees of Telopea, and my brothers kicking a hole in the fibro wall of an old house because they got a bit too excited playing sock-soccer indoors.

My earliest memory of Arabic class is of the teacher leading us in the Arabic equivalent of 'The Wheels on the Bus Go Round and Round', except that my teacher was a Jordanian Palestinian and her word for wheels is the Egyptian word for cupboard. Bus wheels have never looked the same to me since.

From my Arabic language textbooks, I became familiar with Amman Citadel and Baalbek before I ever learned about Egypt's own Qaitbay Citadel or Karnak Temple. And while my cousins played a hand-clapping game called '*Kilo Bamya*' in their school playgrounds, in mine I learned that we 'toot toot' to Beirut and that Abu Salim, yo, yo . . . Well, if you know, you know.

Language and culture of course being intrinsically linked, my parents enforced a 'no English at home' policy. They spoke to me, to their friends and to the local halal butchers and Arab grocers in their native Egyptian dialect of Arabic. And I grew up hearing the replies coming at them in the rich and varied dialects of the Arab world – Libyan, Lebanese, Syrian, Palestinian, Jordanian, Iraqi, Kuwaiti, Algerian, Moroccan, Sudanese, Saudi Arabian, Yemeni, Qatari, Emirati, Ahwaz, Tunisian and so many more – and learning to understand the different phrases and vocabulary.

Learning manifests in different people in different ways. For me, this meant that I learned to mimic the accents of various dialects and to know the differing word usages. Much to the horror of most Egyptians I come across, this has also meant that my Arabic is a bizarre mix of words borrowed from different dialects and an accent that could at best be described as 'globally Arabic' when I am not deliberately putting effort into filtering one sole accent through.

I remember being interviewed by SBS Arabic Radio once in Arabic about an Arab-Australian publication. After the interview went live, I received a telephone call from my Lebanese *tante*, who is married to my Egyptian uncle. 'You sounded more Lebanese than anything in that interview! Why did you do that? You should be proud of your Egyptian heritage!' Her sentiment was – and continues to be – shared by many, no matter the number of times I stress that my Arabic is rarely a conscious, thought-out choice. And while I appreciate my non-Egyptian aunt championing the importance of my Egyptian dialect and its perceived significance to my identity, the answer to her question lies in the hommus-prompted epiphany.

I will forever and always fight for the death of racist stereotypes, and for my right to claim and connect with and bear proudly all the labels that make up the cultural, racial and ethnic flavour of my Melbourne-born, Sydney-raised, Egyptian, African, North-African Arab, Arab-Australian Muslim woman self.

But out of all those labels, when asked about my culture, there is only one that hits closest to home.

I am not as Egyptian as Egyptians expect. I am not as Australian as the pop culture definitions of an Aussie would deem. And there is no part of my cultural upbringing to which any Arab from an Arab country would completely relate.

I am as broadly Arab-Australian as the general, homogenous-sounding label would deem.

Except that, in my case, and the cases of first, second and third generation children of immigrant Arab-Australians, the generic label is uniquely specific.

My Arabness smells of Punchbowl-bought rosewater, backyard-grown-mint tea and Teta Rawheya's *konafa* made from Greek *kataifi*. It's rich with Teta Kareema's stories of times gone by, and of the dulcet recordings of her favourite Abdel Motteleb singing of Cairo love, interrupted by the scratchy, broken-signal broadcasts of Sydney's Arabic radio stations blaring from her room around the clock. My Arabness tastes like Mama's *macarona bachamel* and the Bessemer parties of our youth, and it breathes in stacks of multilingual books and serenity. It is arguments with my *tantes* about the pros and cons of *kibbe nayyeh*, crying through a Nadine Labaki movie, and conversations with friends about race theory and Saleh Bakri. It's coloured by Baba's love for quoting convoluted pre-Islamic Arabic poetry at us, and the red of his yells of 'Speak Arabic!' in the background of all our conversations.

And I do speak it. I speak it through the five different love languages of *konafa*. I speak it through the different marinades in which each Arab culture stews its stuffed grapevine leaves.

I speak it, and sometimes in the form of a blue-label hommus dip can, it speaks back.

Call Me by My Name

Call me by your name.
Call me by my second name.
Because you see my first name
has become synonymous with terrorism

Mohammad,
means praised.

What an overrated title.
Praised be the humble slave
To society,
To the world's whips
to keep my beard in shape;
My tongue in place
Because you're afraid;
of what it can do in front of a microphone.

Because when Muhammad spoke,
he recited poetry.
The Quran is just a holy symphony
that shifted Arabia's sands
Into a tropical oasis.
That demanded woman be equal to man
And to not be complacent
When invaders come for your land;

Protect your language.

You see in English,
You would say my Arabic is broken.

Victim of a generation
that's lost its language
to an education system
that's only spoken white.

Call me by my name.
Call me by my first name.

Zainab
Means blossoming flower.

A creative expression of the world
that continues to curl
and curve
itself to layers of her own mix of
beautiful brown skin.

Just like the Earth
she holds all the
life
inside of her ribs.

Flowers of brightly hued bliss

and a beating drum
that echoes through the chambers of her frame.

But as this masterpiece hung up on the wall,
all she longed for was change.

She wanted it to change so bad,
Each day
took a knife in one hand,
held it against the other,

Strenuously scraped off
All
Her
Colour.

Wondered why she felt incomplete,
A little girl's dream to realise that kind of purity,
That type of cleanliness you would long for
when you're made to feel real,
real dirty.

And slowly swallowed the turpentine
that burned
the hurt off her canvas
like whitening creams.

Only to reveal that she
is bloodless.

Better yet a bloodless coup,
yes this revolution lives in the youth
and resistance of mainstream standards
of who we ought to be.
No more catastrophes,

You see I have a love/hate relationship with poetry.

Because I will write till the sun
becomes the moon,
I can make my words
feel like a sharp-edged knife
even when the English language
is more of a spoon,

Because I know I'm a wordsmith
but I can only write
within
the coloniser's
vocabulary.

I've never written Arabic poetry.

You see I can write words
that could run circles,
                    run races,
        around
You.

Verses that would suffocate your airways
and collapse your lungs,
I can turn my tongue,
Into a rifle.

Aim it at you and make my   shot,
But I'd still be using the invader's weapon,
The Englishman's creation of oppression,
His tool,

And I
Begin to feel like the fool
                                        who woke up
                                                        on the wrong side
                                                of an unholy war.

Is it not ironic to say that the holiest scriptures
Burn like no other?

Even when Arabic is the most beautiful language
and I could manage
to string
a sentence
        or two.

There'd be more weight in a noose.

Despite the culture at my disposal
I am unable

To write something worthy.

How could anything compare to words so holy?

How can the truth be beautiful
and unattractive
at the same time?
So when you look at yourself in the mirror
unsee those lies.
No more paintings of heaven
turned hell.
clear for all to tell
and point out a fake Mona Lisa
when they see one anyway,

Too hard to call us by our names

إسمي مُحَمَّدْ.

My name is Mohammad.

إسمي زَيْنَب.

My name is Zainab.

مُحَمَّدْ.

Mohammad.

زَيْنَب.

Zainab.

مُحَمَّدْ.

Mohammad.

زَيْنَب.

Zainab.

***Zainab Kadhim** is a mixed-raced spoken-word poet and community worker from south-western Sydney. Her works address themes of social justice, female empowerment and self-reflection. After completing her Masters degree in Environmental Change Management, she began working on a sustainability project and now coordinates a storytelling and wellbeing program based in high schools.*

***Mohammad Awad** is a Psychology and Health student at the University of Sydney, working in mental health and striving to destigmatise mental health in diverse communities. As well as being a writer/artist/musician/poet who's running out of ways to express himself, Mohammad is trying to find the best ways to talk about the worst things in life.*

__Michael Mohammed Ahmad__ is the founder and director of Sweatshop: Western Sydney Literacy Movement. He is the award-winning author of The Tribe *(Giramondo, 2014) and* The Lebs *(Hachette, 2018). Mohammed received his Doctorate of Creative Arts from Western Sydney University in 2017.*

The Origin of Leb

On 3 November 1998, while I was travelling to school via Lakemba train station, I spotted a front-page feature in the *Daily Telegraph* which had been put out on display by our local newsagent. The headline of the article read: 'DIAL-A-GUN: Gang says it's easier than buying a pizza'.[1] I was thirteen years old and studying at Punchbowl Boys High School, which was two suburbs over from Lakemba, surrounded by barbed wires and cameras and had a student population of ninety percent Arab and Muslim background. The 'DIAL-A-GUN' article pictured six young men from

1 M. Casey & M. Ogg, 'Dial-a-Gun: Gang says it's easier than buying a pizza', *Daily Telegraph*, 3 November 1998, p. 1.

my school. They were dressed in Fila and Adidas jackets and hoodies; they had menacing and aggressive expressions on their faces, and they each had their fingers crossed in the shapes of letters or cocked in the shape of a gun. 'Members of the Punchbowl Homeboys yesterday demonstrate their call signs,' the photo caption stated.

This newspaper article, which twenty years later continues to fester in my memory, introduced Australia to a unique cultural identity. For the news media, the politicians and the general dominant White culture of Australia, the members of this identity were imagined and constructed as an ancient group who had been imported to Australia from a far-off and unfamiliar place. However, as my Arabian ancestors could tell you, the young men who appeared on the front page of the *Daily Telegraph*, who studied at Punchbowl Boys High School, who wandered the streets of Western Sydney, who were accused of murders and drive-by shootings, implicated in the 2000 Skaf gang rapes, and transformed into international terror suspects after the events of 11 September 2001, were an entirely new cultural group. We called ourselves Lebs. And we originated right here in Australia.

There were two incidents that led to the 'DIAL-A-GUN' article. The first took place on 17 October 1998. A fourteen-year-old boy of Korean background named Edward Lee was stabbed to death in Punchbowl, the result of an altercation between Lee and his three friends and a group who were reported as being a gang of up to twenty young men of 'Middle Eastern appearance' and of 'Lebanese background'.[2] The second took place on 2 November 1998, an overnight drive-by shoot-up of Lakemba police station in which the perpetrators were labelled as 'Middle Eastern appearance' and 'Lebanese background'.[3] My family lived so close to Lakemba police station at the time that I still remember hearing the explosive gunshots which made headlines throughout New South Wales. Even before I saw the news the next day I knew this was going to be called a 'Lebanese' offence – there were so many people from Lebanese background living in Lakemba that we had affectionately come to call the area 'Leb-kemba'.

The aftermath of the murder of Edward Lee and the attack on Lakemba police station was a sensationalised media and political campaign that vilified and demonised Lebanese-Australian communities. Firstly because all people of Lebanese background and/or appearance, particularly young men like me, were now perceived and treated as criminal suspects (with numerous incidents of such young men being harassed by police), and secondly because our broader Lebanese-Australian communities' lack of cooperation with the police, or our genuine inability to aid in tracking down wanted criminals, led some people, especially talk-back radio hosts, to believe that the entire population of citizens from Lebanese backgrounds were colluding and conspiring together, and that our population was therefore inherently criminal.[4]

---

2 J. Collins, G. Noble, S. Poynting & P. Tabar, *Kebabs, Kids, Cops and Crime*, Annandale, NSW: Pluto Press Australia Limited, 2000, p. 1.

3 Collins, Noble, Poynting & Tabar, p. 1.

4 Collins, Noble, Poynting & Tabar, p. 10.

Attitudes such as these in the late nineties failed to recognise the religious, cultural, economic and social diversity of our communities and led to the crude racial stereotyping that became commonplace for Arab-Australians. This included statements made by the NSW Premier at the time, Bob Carr, who was reported in the *Sydney Morning Herald* as saying that the recent disturbances of drugs and car theft were linked to a 'Lebanese gang'.[5] As you can already see, specific to Australia were these examples where the terms 'Lebanese', 'Lebanese background', 'Middle Eastern', 'Middle Eastern background', 'Middle Eastern appearance', 'Arab', 'Arabic-speaking' and 'Muslim' were used interchangeably. In particular the term 'Lebanese' often came to embody any and all 'Arab' and 'Muslim' communities in Australia.

While studying at Punchbowl Boys High School, I hung out with eight young men who all called themselves Lebs, even though three of them had parents who migrated to Australia from Syria, two of them had grandparents from Palestine, one of them had parents from Jordan, one of them had a Lebanese father and an Anglo-Australian mother, and one of them had two parents who were both from Indonesia. I was the only one among them who had two parents and four grandparents originally from Lebanon. Yet despite our incredible diversity as a group, whenever a young woman we were hitting on, or a police officer who pulled us out of a car to check our crotches, or a cab driver who wanted us

---

5 Collins, Noble, Poynting & Tabar, p. 3.

to pay before he drove us to our destination, asked, 'What nasho are ya?' the answer from each of us was always the same, 'Leb'. In this way, you begin to see the emergence of the 'Leb' not as a shorthand Australian way of referring to a foreigner from Lebanon, but as a completely new Australian identity, which contained a set of cultural markers, such as ways of speaking, dressing and walking, which were specific to growing up 'Arab' in Australia.

I immediately recognised the 'Leb' when I saw the 'DIAL-A-GUN' article back in 1998. The photo caption beneath the image indicated that the pictured 'gang' were 'demonstrating their call signs . . . the hand signals are used to communicate simple messages between gang members'.[6] But why, I asked with a scoff, did the boys tell the journalists they were a gang with easy access to guns? Would a serious gang guilty of murder and drive-by shootings really expose themselves in this way to the media, the police, the politicians and the general public? And why, I asked with another scoff, did the journalists who wrote the article and took the photo approach the story so seriously? Would a journalist and newspaper editor have deemed it newsworthy if five Anglo-Australian youths from a North Shore high school had called themselves a homeboy gang?

What was certain to me was that the five 'Lebanese' boys in the 'DIAL-A-GUN' image did not come off as the kind of professional criminal gang that would shoot up police stations and commit murder. This image was more reminiscent of the

6 Casey & Ogg, p. 1.

dress style and physical gestures of African-American hip-hop and gangsta rap artists who had become known to boys like us through the global mass media. In particular, you should consider the so-called 'call signs' used to 'signal messages to other gang members'. Anybody who had shown an interest in African-American hip-hop culture up until the year 1998, which basically included every Arab-Australian male in South-Western and Western Sydney between the ages of ten and twenty-eight, would have recognised that the hand signals of the boys were just emulations of the 'Westside' and 'Eastside' and 'Thug Life' gestures created by rap artists such as Biggie Smalls and Tupac Shakur. The 'Westside' gesture, in which we tucked in the thumb, crossed our centre fingers and spread our outer fingers to make a 'W', originally represented the geographical identities of gangsta rappers such as 2Pac and Outlawz, who were from the West Coast of America. However, although we were often making a direct reference to the African-American rap stars and the American West Coast when flashing the 'Westside' signal, this gesture also began to represent our own marginal Australian identities and geographical identities because the majority of Lebs lived in Sydney's 'West', in suburbs such as Lakemba, Punchbowl, Bankstown, Liverpool, Auburn, Granville, Parramatta and Campbelltown.

What was most ironic about the 'DIAL-A-GUN' article is that while the journalists claimed the boys in the image were flashing unique and coded hand signals to communicate messages, they were also well aware that the boys were simply attempting to mimic African-American hip-hop gangsta culture, stating that, like the 'black homeboy gangs in the United States' the 'Punchbowl Homeboys' wore 'the same baggy jeans, sportswear such as Fila and Adidas, and listen to rap music'.[7] Why then had the journalists interpreted the hand gestures as anything other than a harmless copy?

DIAL-A-GUN

Gang says it's easier than buying a pizza

© Brendan Esposito / Newspix

Whether the journalists were fully aware that the hand signals were just copies of the boys' favourite rap stars or not, they certainly knew, just as the 'Punchbowl Homeboys' knew, that this image and article would terrify and shock the general Australian public. As explained in *Kebabs, Kids, Cops and Crime*: 'This teenage friendship group . . . might have briefly enjoyed their newfound notoriety and the

7 Casey & Ogg, p. 4.

impression of having taken for a ride the credulous reporters of ethnocentric media'.[8] Indeed, you could see from the image itself that the boys were having a laugh at the journalists while playing out their ghetto gangsta fantasies.[9]

I would like to draw your attention to one boy in the photo, standing second from the right, who was bearing a large and innocent-looking smile across his dark-olive complexion and making the gesture of a gun with his fingers – clearly not the same as having cocked an actual gun! Rather than simply *being* the media stereotype, we see here how the 'Leb' consciously *performed* the media stereotype. A female colleague of mine who studied at the Newtown High School of Performing Arts in the late nineties and only dated Lebs during that time helped me understand the appeal of playing the gangsta: 'You guys were so hot. All the boys in my class were terrified of you'.

However, in the case of 'DIAL-A-GUN', it wasn't just young Arab-Australian Muslim men from Western Sydney who were playing out their fantasies:

> The boys in the photo – who are today either engaged in university or further education study or in small business – were posed by the *Telegraph*'s journalist to look the part: they were asked to make hand signals around and look mean.[10]

---

8 Collins, Noble, Poynting & Tabar, p. 2.

9 Collins, Noble, Poynting & Tabar, pp. 45–46.

10 Collins, Noble, Poynting & Tabar, p. 2.

While it was the intention of the 'Punchbowl Homeboys' to emulate their Afro-American subaltern heroes, the intention of the journalists was to exploit these young men's ghetto gangsta fantasies in order to propagate their own White Australian fantasy about the increasing threat of ethnic gangs in Sydney. The article's explicit references to Australian-born boys as 'Lebanese', and its claims that ethnic crime and violence were on the rise in Sydney's south-western suburbs, namely Lakemba and Punchbowl, exposed a deliberate campaign by the dominant culture to vilify and demonise Arab-Australian communities within a colony that had constantly constructed itself as 'White-and-worried'.[11]

Twelve months after Lebs had made their debut appearance in the *Daily Telegraph*, Australian media outlets were set to stereotype, racialise, ethnicise and marginalise us on an unprecedented scale. It was the year 2000 and a group that came to be known as the notorious 'Skaf Gang', which included three young men from my high school, Punchbowl Boys, were convicted for the coordinated gang rapes of several young Anglo-Australian women. Gang leader Bilal Skaf received a controversial fifty-five-year jail sentence for his role in the crimes – the highest ever for an offender of this kind, and 'more than most murderers receive'.[12] As you will see from various case studies, during the allegations, trials, convictions and aftermath, Bilal

---

11 G. Hage, *White Nation: Fantasies of White Supremacy in a Multicultural Society*, Annandale, NSW: Routledge, 1998, pp. 10–11.

12 S. Poynting, G. Noble, P. Tabar & J. Collins, *Bin Laden in the Suburbs*, Annandale, NSW: Sydney Institute of Criminology, 2004, p. 135.

Skaf and thirteen other members of his gang, who were all Australian, were continuously labelled in news headlines and texts as men of 'Lebanese', 'Middle Eastern' and 'Muslim' identity. Journalists, politicians and writers also repeatedly expounded the myth that the rapists were brought up to regard their 'White', 'Western' and 'Caucasian' victims as 'sluts', positioning Arab and Muslim communities in Australia as 'anti-Aussie', 'anti-White' and 'anti-Western'.

Among the numerous articles and news reports covering the Skaf gang rapes between 2000 and 2002 were the recurring commentaries of conservative media journalist Miranda Devine. In an article in the *Sydney Morning Herald* titled, 'Racist rapes: Finally the truth comes out', Devine framed the public debate about the crimes as racism *by* Arab-Muslims rather than racism *against* Australians who happened to be of Arab and Muslim background:

> So now we know the facts, straight from the Supreme Court, that a group of Lebanese Muslim gang rapists from south-western Sydney hunted their victims on the basis of their ethnicity and subjected them to hours of degrading, dehumanising torture. The young women, and girls as young as 14, were 'sluts' and 'Aussie pigs', the rapists said. So now that some of the perpetrators are in jail, will those people who cried racism and media 'sensationalism' hang their heads in shame? Hardly.[13]

---

13 M. Devine, 'Racist rapes: Finally the truth comes out', *Sydney Morning Herald*, 14 July 2002. http://www.smh.com.au/articles/2002/07/13/1026185124700.html [accessed 25 July 2015].

Devine's opening paragraph attempted to reverse the claims that racism towards Arab-Australians and Muslims was fuelling reportage on the gang rapes with a counterclaim that the crimes were racist acts perpetrated by 'Lebanese' and 'Muslims'. This seemed to suggest that because 'racist' comments were made by the perpetrators during their crimes, the reportage of the crimes could not in its own right be racist. However, it did not seem clear why one had to make an either/or argument here – that either the media was being racist towards Arab-Australian Muslims or that Arab-Australian Muslims were guilty of hate crimes and 'racist rapes'. Devine's own article demonstrated perfectly that these two forms of racism could co-exist. On the one hand, the Skaf Gang referring to their Anglo-Australian victims as 'Aussie pigs' during the assaults was racist, and at the same time it was racist when Devine referred to the Australian-born perpetrators of the crimes as 'Lebanese' – intentionally positioning them as foreign and alien within their own nation.

Ten years after the Skaf Gang had been prosecuted for their crimes, Devine continued to release articles of the same nature, one on 15 May 2011 reporting that, 'The gang rapists, Australian-born Lebanese Muslims roamed Sydney hunting for non-Muslim teenage girls they regarded as "Aussie sluts"'.[14] Here we saw a slight evolution in Devine's rhetoric, having adopted the term 'Australian-born' to refer

14 M. Devine, 'Survivor of total horror', *Daily Telegraph*, 15 May 2011. http://www.dailytelegraph.com.au/news/opinion/survivor-of-total-horror/story-e6frezz0–1226055866246 [accessed 25 July 2015].

to the perpetrators. However, her sentence was structured in such a way as to suggest that the rapists, though Australian-born, were still and foremost 'Lebanese', and to construct 'Muslim' identity as inherently foreign. One could ask why Devine, writing an Australian newspaper article for Australian readers, needed to mention the cultural, racial and religious backgrounds of the perpetrators at all if indeed she considered them 'Australian'. The term 'Australian-born' became a rhetorical device to distance the perpetrators' identities from the identity of Australia's dominant cultural groups, a way of saying, 'Sure, they are Australian-born but they are not really Australian like you and me'. This could be best understood as part of what Ghassan Hage called the 'White nation fantasy' – the imaginary position of 'White Australian' was the only position considered *actually* Australian by members and groups from the dominant culture.[15] Hage's concept might have been especially applicable to Devine's sense of Australianness, because her American-born heritage technically made her less Australian than the 'Australian-born Lebanese Muslim' gang rapists she repeatedly attempted to de-Australianise. After reading numerous articles by Devine, I discovered that for some Australians, imagining oneself as 'White' constituted Australianness far more than imagining one's self as 'Australian-born'.

In an essay titled, 'From Centenary to Olympics: Gang rape in Sydney', Kate Gleeson explored how racialising

15 Hage. p. 18.

specific Australian gang rapes up until the year 2000 had been a trope in Sydney's history. She drew parallels between the reports on Irish-Australian gang rapes in 1887 and the gang rapes that had been dominating news headlines in Sydney at the turn of the millennium:

> The Mt. Rennie case of 1887, perpetrated by 20 young men of Irish Catholic descent who were white 'natives' of Australia, exemplifies the long history of gang rape in Sydney. In both the Mt. Rennie and Skaf cases, responses were remarkably uniform and wholly inadequate. In both, the problem of gang rape was identified as a problem of the rapists' 'communities' rather than of the greater society in which they resided. [16]

Gleeson's research was particularly important because it recognised a historical cycle from members of Australia's dominant White culture to actively racialise minority groups in Australian news media and in public and political discourse. This could be contrasted to incidents such as the brutal gang rape and murder of Anita Cobby in 1986. Similar to the Skaf gang rapes in 2000, the reportage on Anita Cobby's murder was linked to the Western Sydney location where the crime was committed and the Western Sydney origins of the perpetrators. However, not mentioned in the reportage was the 'ethnic' background

---

16 K. Gleeson, 'From Centenary to the Olympics: Gang rape in Sydney', *Current Issues in Criminal Justice*, vol. 16, no. 2, 2004, p. 183.

of the men who committed the crime, which happened to be the same Irish heritage as the perpetrators in the Mt. Rennie case of 1887. It has been argued that Anita Cobby's murder was not seen as an 'ethnic crime', and politicians and newspapers did not refer to the incident as an 'Irish crime', because one hundred years on, 'the Irish are now seen as part of the Anglo-Celtic majority'.[17] The normalisation of Irish communities into White Australia which occurred between 1887 and 1986 is significant because it demonstrates that Whiteness is not defined by skin colour or country of origin, nor is it a fixed position. Rather it is a form of capital that can be acquired and accumulated by any cultural group at any point in time.

Throughout the thirty-two and a half years that I have been an Australian, I have never once heard of any police officer or politician or media personality call for Irish community leaders in Australia to intervene whenever the perpetrator of a crime happened to be of Irish descent, whilst at the same time Arab-Muslim community leaders (including myself) have always been expected in Australia to take part of the responsibility and participate in the resolution whenever people of Arab and Muslim backgrounds perpetrated serious crimes. [18] Take for example, the comments made by Devine in her 'Racist rapes' article concerning the racial vilification of all Arab-Australian Muslim males.

---

17 Collins, Noble, Poynting & Tabar, p. 9.

18 Collins, Noble, Poynting & Tabar, pp. 6–7.

> Yes, it is unfair that the vast bulk of law-abiding Lebanese Muslim boys and men should be smeared by association. But their temporary discomfort may be necessary so that the powerful social tool of shame is applied to the families and communities that nurtured the rapists, gave them succour and brought them up with such a hatred of Australia's dominant culture and contempt for its women.[19]

Devine downplayed the impact of racial vilification in the media on Arab-Australian Muslim men (and what she ignored completely, the impact on Arab-Australian Muslim women). What Devine described as simply a 'temporary discomfort' was recognised by Abdallah as 'traumatising' to some Australians of Middle Eastern background,[20] and it was argued by Posetti that public assaults on Muslims were found to be linked to the 'biased' media coverage.[21] Eighteen years on, I still carry with me some extremely painful memories regarding several violent incidents in which White-Australian men physically and verbally attacked me and my fellow Muslim brothers and sisters because of our appearance. I remember taking my three younger sisters to Bondi Beach for some ice cream shortly after the first

19 Devine, 'Racist rapes'.

20 M. Abdallah, 'Muslims in Australia: Negative views and positive contributions', in H. Rane, J. Ewart and M. Abdalla (eds.), *Islam and the Australian News Media*, Melbourne, Vic.: Melbourne University Press, 2010, p. 27.

21 J. Posetti, 'Jihad sheilas or media martyrs? Muslim women and the Australian media', in H. Rane, J. Ewart & M. Abdalla (eds.), *Islam and the Australian News Media,* Melbourne, Vic.: Melbourne University Press, 2010, pp. 80–81.

round of media reports about 'Lebanese' rapists had been circulated. Four White men, who were translucent and oily against the night shadows of the ocean, began to howl at us. 'How would *you* like it if we gang-banged *your* bitches, ya sand nigger,' one of the men hissed at me.

In addition to downplaying the severity and impact of racial vilification, Devine's rhetoric also attributed the blame for the gang rapes, and the responsibility to take action in response to them, not just to the perpetrators of the crimes but also to the 'families' and 'communities' of those perpetrators. When reading Devine's article for the first time, her comments made me wonder: would she have shamed and blamed the communities and families of rapists in Australia who came from Irish and British heritage?

One of the most detailed accounts of the Skaf gang rapes made its appearance, ten years on, in popular Australian literature. The true crime novel *Evil in the Suburbs* was written by Cindy Wockner, the *Daily Telegraph*'s legal affairs editor who led the paper's coverage of the rapes, and Michael Porta, the detective sergeant who linked together a series of rapes across South-Western Sydney, ultimately leading police to the Skaf Gang.[22] The cover of *Evil in the Suburbs* featured mugshots of gang leader Bilal Skaf and his younger brother, Mohammed Skaf. Particularly striking was the image of Bilal, bearing a large grin that

22 C. Wockner & M. Porta, *Evil in the Suburbs*. Australia: Random House, 2010.

exposed his small crooked white teeth. The combination of the title and the unremorseful mugshots served to reinforce the common tropes mainstream news media had already generated in Australia, which synonymised men of Middle Eastern appearance with the western suburbs of Sydney and 'evil'.

The first time I saw *Evil in the Suburbs* was during my second year at Western Sydney University, Bankstown Campus, which had the largest percentage of Muslim university students in the country. Over one hundred copies of the book had been placed on a stand at the entrance of the Co-op Bookshop. As soon as it caught my gaze, I grabbed a copy and took it straight to the counter – anxious to read the first Australian novel I had ever seen with people who looked like me on the cover. A middle-aged White woman, with bright blue eyes, dry tanned skin and straight silver hair scanned the book for me. 'Do you know if this book is fair-minded?' I asked her.

'I cried so much when I read what yous did to those girls,' she responded.

For starters, I read the blurb on the back cover of *Evil in the Suburbs*. It promised that this was the 'first time' we would be told the 'gripping full story of the gang rapes', which included 'personal stories of the young women who had the courage to report the crimes', and how the police 'tracked down the perpetrators'. Then, over the next week, I read the book from cover to cover twice over. I needed to understand why the White woman had implicated me in the gang rapes, why she said 'yous' instead of 'they'.

As both a 'novel' and a 'true account', *Evil in the Suburbs* was written from an open third-person perspective which attempted to detail the factual events and dates surrounding the Skaf gang rapes and the prosecution of the gang rapists, while also taking the reader into the emotional and psychological experiences of the key figures, especially the victims, involved in the crimes. The first chapter, 'Power', for example, detailed sexual assault victim Natalie Vickers' day in court, while moving in and out of recollections involving the fourteen boys who had lured her to a Western Sydney park, pinned her, and took turns raping her while the others looked on and laughed.[23]

In addition to the gang rape victims, the perspectives in *Evil in the Suburbs* also focused on the gang rapists themselves. For example, the fourth chapter, 'The Family Skaf', described the appearance of gang rapists Bilal and Mohammed Skaf's home, 'a modest three-bedroom weatherboard cottage nestled in Greenacre', and the contents within their bedroom, an 'Aladdin's cave of goodies, the ill-gotten spoils of their extracurricular activities'.[24] These orientalist descriptions seemed to simplify the unique Lebanese-Australian Western Sydney identities of the Skaf brothers into Arab caricatures: Ali-Baba-type thieves one might find in *Tales from the Thousand and One Nights*.

23 Wockner & Porta, p. 3.

24 Wockner & Porta, p. 17.

In the same chapter, the authors also drew reference to a journey Bilal Skaf had made to Lebanon in 1998.[25] Wockner and Porta carefully insinuated that it was Bilal's time in his parent's country of origin that influenced his criminal behaviour in Australia: 'Whatever happened to him in Lebanon, not long after Bilal returned to Australia he graduated from minor crime to big league player'.[26] This kind of speculative language – 'whatever happened' – was a cheap but effective literary device; Lebanon was implicated in the crimes of Australian citizens even though there was no evident connection between Lebanon and the crimes themselves. While implicating Lebanon, the device also absolved Australia of responsibility – *it was not Australians committing these crimes, it was the foreigners with foreign values who happened to live in Australia committing them.*

While implicating Lebanon in the Skaf gang rapes, I also found several examples in *Evil in the Suburbs* that attempted to implicate the broader Lebanese-Australian population in the crimes. Chapter two, for example, was titled 'Family Ties'. The heading itself cleverly suggested that the Skaf gang's activities were knotted into a familial and communal network of criminality. Within the chapter was a description of the Skaf home which zoomed in on a picture in the living room of Bilal 'arrogantly holding a large military-style rifle in one hand and a shining handgun in the other'.[27]

25 Wockner & Porta, p. 21.

26 Wockner & Porta, p. 21.

27 Wockner & Porta, p. 8.

Although this was a well-known image of Bilal Skaf which had been circulated by several newspapers and TV news networks in 2000, there was no evidence to suggest that the image was being proudly displayed in the Skaf family living room at the time of the gang rapes. By situating the image in such a way in their book, Wockner and Porta seemed to be suggesting that Bilal's tendencies toward violence and aggression were unashamedly endorsed and celebrated by his family and community members. This insinuation paralleled Miranda Devine's claims some years earlier that the families and cultural/religious groups 'nurtured the rapists, gave them succour and brought them up with hatred',[28] and the observation that a broader Australian society came to perceive the entire 'Lebanese community' as colluding and conspiring with one another, fashioning a culture that was inherently criminal.[29]

A handful of pages into *Evil in the Suburbs*, Wockner and Porta began to paint their portrait of evil in the

28 Devine, 'Racist rapes'.

29 Collins, Noble, Poynting & Tabar, p. 10.

suburbs: 'Near Punchbowl High School, a passing car slowed down and a group of Middle Eastern boys emerged and surrounded the by now frightened young girl'.[30] This statement seemed to deliberately downplay the rapists' Australian identities and amplify their Arab identities in contrast to 'actual' Australians. What exactly made these boys Middle Eastern instead of Australian? Why not just call them 'a group of boys'? From a literary perspective, 'Middle Eastern' became an effect, a device that enabled you to distinguish racially between 'evil' and 'innocent'. Wockner and Porta also referred to 'Punchbowl High School' in this passage. They most likely meant Punchbowl Boys High School, seeing as it was the only high school in Punchbowl named after the suburb. Here I saw how particular locations in Sydney became literary effects too, devices that enabled you to distinguish geographically between the 'safe' and the 'dangerous'. Punchbowl, and more broadly Western Sydney, was often connected with Middle Eastern crime, and crime in general, in Australian politics, media, film and literature. This was because Western Sydney was positioned as Sydney's geographical other, primarily due to economic and class factors,[31] in much the same way that culturally and linguistically diverse minorities were positioned as Australia's racial other.

The term 'Middle Eastern' in Wockner and Porta's text was particularly striking to me because, unlike the term

---

30 Wockner & Porta, p. 14.

31 D. Powell, *Out West,* St Leonards: Allen & Unwin, 1993, p. xvii.

'Lebanese', it attempted to be a physical description of the rapists as well as a cultural marker, especially through explicit use of the term 'Middle Eastern appearance'.

> Chatting innocently on the phone, Maria looked up. Fear suddenly gripped her. Six boys of Middle Eastern appearance materialised out of the darkness and surrounded her car, like some kind of macabre scene from a kidnap movie. The driver's side door was wrenched open. Before she had time to think, Maria saw the unmistakable flash of a blade knife.[32]

As an author and editor who has acquired ten years of university education in philosophy, cultural studies, literature and creative writing, this type of language did not just bother me because of its racism, it also bothered me because of its incredibly poor literary merits. As a literary device, describing all the men in the scene as 'Middle Eastern appearance' reduced them to cartoons with no distinct individual qualities or traits worth imagining or representing. Even if the men were being represented as a homogenous entity, the term 'Middle Eastern appearance' was ambiguous, because there was no example or trait inherent to the term which enabled readers to see what the appearance looked like, such as a specific skin tone, hair colour or eye colour; and because the six men in the scene emerged from darkness. Within this night-time setting,

32 Wockner & Porta, p. 9.

what aspects of any one of these men, or even all the men as a single formation, made them Middle Eastern in appearance? In 'On Being Lebanese-Australian', Noble and Tabar argued that the media and political representations of Arabic-speaking people in Australia constructed them first as a cohesive community and ethnicity, and then 'criminalised' that ethnicity, so that the criminal act became un-Australian.[33] Now it all made sense: Wockner and Porta's choice of words, 'Middle Eastern', served to construct each Australian male of Arab and Muslim background as a homogenous object, so that whenever a White woman working in a bookshop thought of the Skaf gang, she immediately imagined the rapists in terms of us all – 'yous'.

I finished this essay in the year 2018. And it began in the year 1998. Even after twenty years, it is difficult not to imagine myself, and not to be imagined by fellow Australians, as an ethnic gangster, drug dealer and rapist. These stereotypes did not die down as the years went by, instead they evolved like a 'sand monkey' transforming into a 'sand nigger'. Three years after 'DIAL-A-GUN' introduced Lebs to the Australian mainstream two aeroplanes struck the World Trade Centre in New York City. I remember the morning of September 11, 2001. I woke up from my bed, dressed in Spider-Man pyjamas, and walked into the living room of our home in Lakemba. My parents, siblings, cousins, aunts and uncles sat around the television

33 G. Noble & P. Tabar, 'On being Lebanese-Australian: Hybridity, essentialism, strategy', in G. Hage (ed), *Arab-Australians Today*, Melbourne: Melbourne University Press, 2002, p. 137.

and stared at the news headline on Channel Ten: *America Under Attack*. For most of the world, this was a day that would change all Arabs and Muslims into terrorists. But for me, this was just another incident which added a new label to the origin of Leb. As those two towers crumbled, and as the blood and dust began to spread throughout the world, I remember a faint voice inside my head: '*Allah have mercy, please have mercy*'.

***Hana Assafiri** has dedicated her life to removing barriers that prevent women from living prosperous lives. She opened the Moroccan Soup Bar in North Fiztroy in 1998, which has provided employment opportunities for marginalised members of the community. Hana is the founder of 'Speed Date a Muslim', a community event to combat Islamophobia, and 'Conversation Salons', for academics, journalists and community organisations to discuss women's issues, racism and the need for a progressive vision. In 2017 Hana was inducted into the Victorian Honour Roll of Women and in 2019 Hana was awarded the Order of Australia.*

Islam: Reclaiming the Narrative

Overview

In an increasingly polarised world, governance systems are losing legitimacy; whether it be dictatorships or democracies, their failings are on display around the globe. Fractured social systems that are built on inherent inequality. Systems that subjugate women; systems that exploit the poor and vilify the needy amongst us. Systems that need to continue to create enemies, whose currency is hate and vilification. As the world becomes more and more connected, as women partake in public life in an unprecedented way, systems that are built on our inequality are becoming unsettled.

This as an opportunity to reform and progress societies; instead the unsettled systems have fractured and polarised societies. The promise of a vision where open, plural, fair and responsible societies are possible, empowering and enabling those who have been denied and marginalised, is pitted against existing systems holding on only by returning to the most misogynist colonial rule and repealing the gains made by minorities because they threaten and undermine their dominance. I am a Muslim woman living in the West and trying to navigate a sense of self and identity not defined by others. Reclaiming the principles of Islam which speak to social justice and human rights, compassion, humanity, and provide guidance for these times.

Speech during Ramadan 2019

As-salāmu 'alaykum wa-raḥmatu llāhi wa-barakātuhu. If we for a moment stop to contemplate what those three words mean, *As-salāmu 'alaykum.* Peace be upon you, peace be upon you in order that the Mercy of Allah (*Subhanahu wa ta'ala*) is availed to us. If we look at the global context, not much peace is on offer. Not much peace is on offer in the Muslim world, not much peace is on offer in the Western world. How do we attain peace? How do we live and create environments of harmony and peace?

All my work is with people who acknowledge the context and the climate in which we stand. Almost all events are prefaced with acknowledgement of the continued dispossession of the Indigenous peoples of this country. We welcome, we do amazing dance ceremonies, we do symbolic rhetorical acknowledgement. Very little, however, is impacting behavioural change. If we are committed to achieving peace and truth and justice, we have to be founded on solid foundations. We must advocate speaking truth and justice for all, beginning with the Indigenous peoples of this country. I would love for us to be able to mirror New Zealand's approach as a start. How many of us know how to speak any Indigenous languages?

Surely we should!

In New Zealand, when Prime Minister Jacinda Ardern addresses the nation, it is bilingual. The anthem, the social recognition, the high commissioner: all systems preface events by acknowledging the Indigenous people of the country. They are active in changing the behaviour that is required for true reconciliation and justice and peace of societies.

Australia is now the only Commonwealth country in the world that does not have a treaty with its Indigenous peoples. We cannot continue to ignore this, no matter our causes, and especially as Muslims and as Muslim women. We are living during hostile times; we are living on the margins of society under constant scrutiny, interrogation and suspicion, yet no matter our causes we are the benefactors of the dispossession of the Indigenous people of this country.

Our silence makes us complicit, and unless we actively advocate these causes the outcome will not change.

My life's journey has been shaped by adversity since my early developmental years. And over the course of my life I have found empowerment as a woman, as a feminist, inside Islam by reacquainting myself with an understanding of Islam and Islamic principles relating to women and social justice issues for the times upon us.

Islam is founded on the principle of truth-telling, *Koulu alhaq walow a3la anfousikum*. A concept, a principle of truth, even if you implicate yourself. This is a foundational principle not to be shied away from, no matter how unsettling it might be.

We were saddened by the Christchurch attacks. They were enabled through the very divisive and polarised conversations unfolding around the globe. These seeds of hatred have been sown. This did not happen in isolation; this man, nameless or otherwise, saw himself in the discourse of our governments, he saw himself validated. When we continue to whip up such hysteria about Muslims, and we are silent, this will be the result. All it needs is another dimension of drugs, alcohol, disenfranchisement, mental health for this polarisation to have dire consequences. When we tell the truth about what is unfolding around us and demand to be the custodians of the social values we hold dear. This situation will not fix itself by magic.

The environment upon us is unprecedented, the undercurrent of Islamophobia cuts across the political spectrum. It has global expression and it is reinforced by our media. If we do not have a relationship with Muslims; what resonates is very negative images. There are two reasons for this. There are no Muslim countries across the world adhering to the basic Islamic principles of human rights and social justice. The expressions of Islam that are on show are a departure from those basic foundations. Yes? Can somebody actually name one country, one Muslim country, that adheres to the basic principles of Islam? Islam is founded on, and is a natural ally of, human rights and social justice values. You would be hard-pressed to see an example of that shown anywhere around the globe. Yet by reclaiming Islamic foundations, we are enabled to exist alongside as well as within Western democracies, who by the way have also departed from their very hallmarks of compassion, and of human rights. Western democracies cage people needing compassion. Western democracies who vilify the marginalised, who use the currency of hate on the vulnerable – these societies have departed from those hallmarks of Western civility. So it is not just the Muslim world that has departed from its foundations and principles of Islam, it is the entire globe and we are living in polarised times.

When our leadership says, 'Islam is at odds with Western democracies.' When our leadership is silent about comments like: 'Put them in internment camps'; 'It's okay to be white'; 'We want to limit Muslim migration'; 'They need "The final solution"', when these conversations aggregate, they form an opinion about Muslims and unsettle the society.

We once looked at one another with curiosity, fast forward 20 years or so, we now look at someone different to us with suspicion and fear. Since September 11, the Western world changed for the West and it certainly changed for the Muslim communities.

In the aftermath of Christchurch, the world changed once again for Muslims living in the West. And most Muslims, no matter our political persuasion, weren't surprised. Most of us weren't shocked. Yes, we were saddened, but we weren't shocked because this reality was inevitable, it has been our constant normal. Christchurch is one of the worst historical exportations of a radicalised terrorist since the colonisation and the massacre in this country of Indigenous peoples.

For peace to eventuate, the social systems need to be founded on justice, and justice requires a guardian in truth-telling. In the face of fake news, truth has become a matter of perspective and this has created distrust in our social systems. If, at the level of governance, they are not safe-guarding our social values that enable social harmony, and if the institutions, religious institutions and media beneath our governance are not the guardians in truth-telling and have not maintained relevance, communities become disengaged and distrusting. Especially when religious institutions, with no exception, alienate women, and have severed women from a contribution to the understanding and expression of the faith, where women are relegated to back-door entries behind garbage bins and told to be quiet. For your voices must not be heard. Societies and religious institutions are built on the subjugation of women, whether it be the House of Parliament or the house of God. Surely it's not a competition for misogyny.

Societies cannot progress unless women are empowered. Women are the forefront of shaping social attitudes. When they are subjugated, when they are violated, when they are put down, they will raise a society that is ignorant. Which is what we're seeing unfold around the world.

Islam was revealed during a time when an unequal society needed to be recalibrated towards a system of justice. That is

Islam's message. There is no compulsion in Islam. Nobody's forced to be a Muslim; it is a way of life if we choose it. And if it is chosen, there are a number of guiding principles to inform and enable us to navigate our daily lives.

Islam, unlike other faiths, does not have a hierarchy. There is no pope, no bishop, no priest. Islam provides direct access to Allah; it doesn't require anyone else to validate or legitimise your faith.

Islam was revealed to transform society from the most unequal of systems, which saw the infanticide of girls, the exploitation of the poor and the trading in slavery. Islam called on its *umma* to be knowledgeable, *iqra2*. Read, seek knowledge before you pray and believe in the other pillars. Islam invites you to scrutinise and challenge what you think you know. It is stated that only those who are truly knowledgeable will appreciate and understand and express Islam.

Islamic expressions have been confounded with culture and tradition and are far removed from Islamic principles of peace, and love, and justice, and human rights. No country around the world equates Islam with those values. And it is upon us to reject the nonsensical associations and that we all have an incentive to challenge our politicians, our media. Our citizenship can no longer be complacent. Active citizenship – they are us – we have to see our freedom tied to the liberation of others. This is the sort of society we are putting our hands up to say, 'I will live in these circumstances or not'.

Founded on culture and tradition and so far removed from Islamic principles. If we bring it back to measuring Islam and its principles of peace and justice and human rights, no conversation around the globe at the moment equates us to those values. And it is upon us to reject, and continue to reject, if we are to advocate for more harmonious societies.

This commitment has to be more than paying lip service. We all have to find our voice when our politicians speak against the values of plurality and respect; we have to make it our business to speak out. That is the society we are putting our hands up for. Active citizenship is what is required to live in these circumstances.

Ramadan, simply, is an opportunity to reaffirm those Islamic values. It's an opportunity for Muslims and non-Muslims to come together and to connect. And for Muslims it is to transcend our egos. Not often do we find ourselves, even Muslims, understanding the principle meaning behind Ramadan. We equate it, unfortunately and sadly, mainly only with food, yet food is the smallest part of Ramadan. Ramadan is about transcending our need for gratification. It is a time where we recognise that the ego (in all societies) is probably one of the most dangerous human elements we all possess. And Ramadan enables us the opportunity to discipline and to train the ego and refrain from the need for instant gratification, from all temptation and desire, including food. The benefits of Ramadan are cumulative and give us the opportunity to re-engage our capacity with humanity and connect with the plight of others. When we transcend, and put a little bit of distance between our need to gratify – what we need right now – this results in our ability to better engage with the needs of others.

There is one profound tension between Islam and the Western worldview. There is an undercurrent conversation that there is a clash of civilizations. That Islam has no place in the Western modern world because its ideology is backward and it needs reformation. As a Muslim woman, a feminist, human rights activist and advocate, I have found utmost empowerment within Islam as a society that affords dignity and respect to its citizens, a society that takes responsibility for the socially vulnerable and asks us to be responsible for our privileges. Islam compels us to take on the causes of those who have been marginalised – no matter who they are – Indigenous people, the gay community, the environment advocates, asylum seekers, the homeless. We are compelled as Muslims to take on those causes and take up our civil responsibility.

So where are tensions? When Muslims butt up against a system of injustice there will be tensions. When the environment around us is just and fair, the principles of Islam are actually consistent with those environments and this will enable the social harmony we all seek.

There is, however, one other thing that, as Muslims, our expression of freedom differs to that of Western expressions, which I just want to briefly touch on.

For the sake of clarity I will over simplify this point, Western civilisation measures its expression of freedom through its ability to fulfill and gratify all desires. The freer we are, the more we can express our need for immediate and instant gratification. This expression becomes enshrined in law and all the social institutions. Our progress and reform of our social systems lean more and more towards our hedonistic expression. Even our ability to express bigoted and harmful views is seen as a right not to be regulated or censored. And we are seeing the failings of those systems unfolding around the world.

By contrast, for Muslims our freedom is expressed through reigning in and disciplining our need for gratification.

Lora Inak *was born in Istanbul, Turkey, during a period of civil unrest. Her parents, Assyrian Orthodox Christians, made the difficult decision to find a safer place to live. That's how, aged four, Australia became her home. She began her writing journey with middle grade and picture book texts, but finally found publishing success with her first YA novel,* Unspoken Rules.

One of a Kind

I shuffle into the front pew and lower myself down, the cool wooden surface solid against the backs of my shaking legs. The teardrop-shaped chandeliers cast a soft light over the congregation, but the mood is dim. Framed depictions of Jesus Christ at his birth, his crucifixion and resurrection adorn every wall. Life. Death. Life again.

She's dead now. Will she live again?

Tear ducts raw, I clutch my eulogy as if it were a life raft in a roaring black sea. Shoulders press against mine, hands stroke my back. I can hear shuffling and crying and whispering. '*Aleawd Bisalamtikun,*' they say to me in Arabic, their eyes full of pity. '*Basiniz Sagolsun,*' they murmur in Turkish.

Spicy incense fills my nose. Bells tinkle in my ears. I am surrounded by so many people in this solemn place . . . a place I've been hundreds of times before. I don't come much anymore.

Just keep your eyes down. It might all be a dream.

He takes my hand, my Australian husband. The hairs on his wrist tickle mine. He whispers something kind. I don't know what. I'm inside me, holding my torn-up heart.

I thought she'd be angry at me, for wanting to be with a man outside the community, for daring to travel a different road. But she wasn't. She was happy, glad that the sacrifices she'd made meant I'd be able to marry for love.

A deep melancholy twang silences the room. It's followed by another, and another. Each sadder and lonelier than the last. It's coming from behind the red curtains.

It snatches the breath from my lungs.

As the hollow, wooden sounds ring with loss and hammer nails of agony into my heart, I remember her still smiling. Her long thin arms raised above her head, her fingers clicking with joy, her big-toothed smile stretching all the way to her eyes. Those eyes that used to be full of light and fire and life.

Near the end, they were dull and yellowed. Scared.

My chest tightens, the sorrow I've held down rising to the surface, washing over me. Drowning me again. I can't breathe. I cover my face, press my fingers into my sockets to stop the tears. I groan, wet drops flowing down my face and off my chin. Strong arms wrap around me. They're warm and assuring. Familiar. He smells of earth and sweat and home. But he doesn't understand. How can he? He hasn't lost yet.

Stop crying. Stop it. She never did. She was never weak. Even when her body was dying, she didn't cry.

I grit my teeth, swallow down the burning bile in my throat and try to block the memories flooding in. They make me so sad now.

I was seven years old when my dog died. Run over by a car. I screamed at the sight of his curled, crumpled body. She loved Max too. He was hers, but she didn't cry or scream like me. She swallowed hard, picked him up and took him away.

The rustle of taffeta draws my eyes to the dividing curtains. I keep my gaze to the right, away from that long dark wooden box. I haven't seen it, but I know it's there. I can feel its black presence.

She can't be in there. She'd never stay still for that long. Be confined. This is just a bad dream.

It's Zaven, her musician friend. He's on the altar, seated with the pear-shaped oud propped on his knee. His eyes are shut tight, his back bowed over the instrument, his right hand strumming the strings. He remembers, just like I do, how much she loved his music. Loved to dance the *Diyarbakir halay*, her arms waving about, her feet kicking the air. He remembers all those nights we spent at his tavern eating skewered lamb and cheese pide, eggplant dip with warm Turkish bread, gossiping, jesting and laughing. She was the brightest, loudest of all the women, slapping friends on the back, a cigarette dangling from her mouth, a glass of whisky and cola in her hand. She wasn't meek or obedient or dainty like she was meant to be. She was forceful, and active, and opinionated. She had thoughts. She had important ideas.

A picture flashes in my mind. It's quick, but brutal. She's lying limp on that hospital bed, decayed, fighting for air. My heart jolts. No more jesting, or laughing, or dancing. Her lungs were all but gone. Blackened.

Listen. This music is for her. If she could hear it, she'd be so happy. She might even smile again. For so long, she didn't smile.

The last few chords echo across the nave and fade like the dying sun. Slowly he rises, her musician friend, cradling the oud to his heart, his eyes wet, his face pale. With heavy steps, he shuffles into a pew beside his family.

Everyone is silent.

She would have applauded him. Whistled and yelled out for more. Made a big racket to make sure everyone appreciated him like she did. It reminds me of the time in my teen years when I played competitive netball. I was landing goal after goal, pushing myself hard, eager to win. Her eyes sparkled with pride on the sidelines. She clapped and whistled, called out my name with her Middle Eastern accent, and added a few Turkish chants just to make sure everyone heard. She laughed at me when I turned red, told me I shouldn't be embarrassed of my family, my language.

My eyes slip to the left, to that rectanglular box. My nose stings.

Father Aphrem takes the pulpit wearing his black robes, phiro on his head, eyes soft and kind. He knew her. She used to come to this church, but she never really believed. Not in his version of God anyway. She was expected to believe, and she tried to. She definitely tried, but I knew she didn't. It irked her that women weren't allowed up there too. Up on the altar. Running the show. They were expected to sit quietly in the pews, mantillas on their heads, hands clasped obediently beside their husbands and children. Then, afterwards, they were supposed to go to the kitchen and prepare the coffee and food. She didn't like that. She would rather have been talking politics with the men, sharing her thoughts on how to best run the church.

She's up on the altar now. Right near the pulpit where she was never allowed in life. Only in death.

I can imagine her rolling her eyes at the irony. She didn't abide by gender norms in our community. It wasn't anything deliberate, just something inside her that pushed her a different way. She had passions and interests and ideas that were considered 'male'. She used to build wooden cabinets with nothing but the simplest tools and a curious mind. She fixed appliances and decorated the house each Christmas with an amazing array of lights. The kind neighbours made a special effort to come and see. She loved her car, cared for it like a child. I watched her, unaware at the time she was unconventional, soaking it all in, understanding deep down that women didn't have to fit a mould . . . that they were just as clever and capable as men.

Father Aphrem reads passages from the Bible in Arabic, his tone lifting and dipping, his words guttural yet melodic. I never learned Arabic, and my Turkish wasn't great either.

She used to shake her head and tut when I couldn't remember the language. When I'd reply in English instead.

She ignored me, feigned deafness until I spoke to her in our mother tongue. She'd tell me never to forget where I was from, to be proud of it. But back then, I wasn't proud. I didn't want to be different.

Assembled inside the chancel, the choir sing sombre notes. I listen, picturing her watching us. She'd probably say that the choir needs more practice, that they needed to get better at singing as a group. She'd point out that the aisle should be vacuumed and that the clerestory could do with some glass cleaner, a squeegee and someone with a good eye for perfection like her. She'd tell me that my black dress is too big on me, and that my hair needs a comb. I'd raise my eyebrows, hands on hips, and tell her that my dress fitted just fine a week ago. It's just that . . . since then I've lost interest in food.

The choir finishes and shuffles into their seats. I clutch my paper, heart quickening. It's almost my turn. My stomach clenches.

I can't do this. She'll be disappointed if I lose my spot, or forget parts, or just stand there in front of people and stammer. Just like that time when I played the centipede in my grade 5 school production of *James and the Giant Peach*.

She made me the most amazing costume with wire and foam and chocolate brown fabric. She stayed up all night, three nights in a row to finish it. Made everyone else's look hacked together. So the principal asked her if she could make everyone else's costume too. That was the first time I was truly proud of her. Didn't care that she couldn't speak

English, or that she didn't dress like the other mums. I was chuffed to stand beside her on stage, after the performance, when they gave her flowers and a gift for her help.

Father Aphrem looks down at me, nodding. My heart stills and every muscle in my body turns to ice.

My throat is thick with grief. How can I stand beside that box and speak when I know she's in there? Still. Cold. Dead.

Darkness edges my eyes. He strokes my hand again, my tall gentle man. 'Do it for her,' he tells me.

And that's when I see her, inside my head, behind my eyes. Her slim frame, tall and strong. Her skin rosy now. Her hair shiny. She looks at me and somehow I know she's here, in this room, waiting to hear me. Listening to what I wrote about her. She holds out her hand, and I rise to my feet, suddenly full of purpose. I walk to the altar, my heart thrumming, my lungs inning and outing. I stop just before the steps, right beside her in that box.

I wasn't there in her final minutes. When she needed me most. I wasn't beside her then. I was racing to get to her. Sobbing behind the wheel. Knowing I might never see her again in this life. Hating every traffic light, beeping and cursing at people I've never met.

For a moment I lose courage. My shoulders drop and I want to run. The thought of her lifeless body, sheathed in a white sheet, burning me up inside.

I should have been there. I should never have left her that night, when she called out after me. My name, the last thing she ever said. My son would have been okay. One night without me would have been fine . . . but I couldn't just leave him. I felt responsible; my deep sense of duty inherited from my father.

I blink back my tears, lift my shoulders and look over the sea of loving faces. There's my wilted father in the front row, his wrinkles deepened with loss. He's beside my sisters, trying to hold himself together. He's never been afraid to cry, afraid to show weakness. He's always been okay with sharing his hurt, his fears. He was the one who kissed me when I was down and taught me to ride my bike. He let me walk on his back when I was little and threw me into a swimming pool to teach me to swim. He is quiet and gentle and hardworking. I'm like him. But I'm more like her.

Be brave. She was brave, and tough. All the way to the end. Do this for her . . . and do it well. Make her proud one last time.

My heart surges. I turn to that long dark box. I'm not afraid of it anymore. Her body is in there, but she is not. Not really. She's somewhere else. With God perhaps. In heaven, I hope. Maybe right beside me for the next little while.

I unfold my paper, smooth out the crumpled parts, my first word catching in my throat.

She's looking at me now. Waiting. I won't let her down. I'll be strong. This is for her.

I take a deep breath and begin. I tell the congregation that my mother was one of a kind. For an Assyrian woman of her era, living in Turkey, she was different. She was strong when women were expected to be weak. She was fearless when women were meant to be protected. She was proud, and capable . . . a complex fabric of colours and textures. Unique, unconventional . . . a trailblazer.

She left her family behind, travelled to an island on the other side of the world and started a new life. In the new world, she never lost sight of who she was or where she'd come from, even when she was made to feel alien, unwelcome.

She could do, or be, anything.

When I finish, I look up, my eyes resting on my father. I see his tears flowing like rain, his skin marked with age, his eyes dulled with grief. He knew her best. Sometimes they clashed. Often, she didn't back down.

I wait for my heart to settle.

My mother pushed me hard, expected me to be my best. I didn't always live up to her high standards, but I know that I'll be eternally grateful. She bestowed on me the gifts of independence, fierce determination and a belief I could do and be anything. She taught me to be proud of who I am, for all the things that make me different, like my black hair and crooked nose, my unique take on the world along with my quirks and odd sense of humour, my talents, strengths, and all the things I've inherited from my rich heritage.

I fold my eulogy and hold it tight in my hand. I didn't break down crying or forget any important parts.

Maybe . . . she heard me. Maybe she's proud.

I turn to that rectangle vessel, the one that will take her away forever. I run my hand down its length. It's cool. Smooth. I'm not dreaming. She's gone. But I'll never forget her.

Ever.

Omar Bensaidi is a researcher investigating what political activism means in a Digital Age. He is interested in questions of race, social justice and digital technologies and their intersections in contemporary society. Growing up in Western Sydney to migrant parents of Algerian and Taiwanese backgrounds, Omar has written about his views and experiences in The Guardian *and* Right Now.

Of 'Middle-Eastern Appearance'

In one of my first encounters with the New South Wales police force, I was stopped on suspicion of committing a crime. Apparently I fit the description of a criminal: white jumper, black pants and white shoes – quite a generic sketch, it would seem. 'That's it, Officer? A hundred people in this area fit that description – why me?' I challenged.

'Listen, mate, I may be generalising, but I suspect you of the crime, do you got a problem with that?' he replied.

'I think you're being a bit racist, don't you think?'

When I said this his eyes lit up and the veins on his forehead pulsated. 'I may be stereotyping, or being racist, but I don't give a fuck. A crime has been committed and you're the suspect.' And then it hit me. Maybe for him, being labelled a racist wasn't as derogatory as we currently imagined it to be. Maybe within the force it was a medal proudly worn alongside the police badge.

Two weeks ago I was threatened with being shot in the back for committing the indictable crime of 'jaywalking'. My friends and I had driven fifteen minutes to Sydney's Eastern Suburbs for dinner at a restaurant we frequently visited. But this meal would be different. As we crossed the road an undercover police car skidded around the corner, cutting us off, attempting to move us off the road. What followed was an intense questioning; it was apparent that jaywalking wasn't our only crime that night.

'What are you guys doing here?' the officer shouted from within the car. 'You guys seem to be a far way from home.' Without accusing us of a crime, the police officer continued questioning our reason for visiting his area, as if our presence had tainted this neighbourhood. I realised then that maybe my Australian citizenship was restricted to Western Sydney.

'You may as well have shot us, instead of trying to run us over with your car,' I said sarcastically.

The officer was having none of it. If my mere presence wasn't enough, here I was spoiling the air with my words. He looked at me dead in the eye: 'Why don't you turn around, run off, and maybe I will'.

Immediately visions of Walter Scott being gunned down as he ran away from an officer in South Carolina rushed through my mind. I had no intention of testing the officer's resolve. Being suspected of no crime and not being under arrest, I decided to turn around and slowly walk away in the hope of ending the encounter. His voice followed after me, demanding I continue the engagement. I turned around to see the officer clutching at his pistol strapped into his waist belt. He tilted his head towards the gun, 'I'm not done with you yet'. He was eager to keep true to his threat, it seemed.

I was humiliated and frightened. Still, I could not claim to be entirely surprised. I understood where this was coming from. Facing police racism was not an unusual occurrence, and this interaction was by no means exceptional. In fact, interactions with police authorities had ceased being exceptional long ago and now merely reinforced my powerlessness in the face of such a racist behemoth. It reminded me – in case I had foolishly forgotten – of my true place in this society. This particular interaction was simply the latest in a long line to be neatly filed away in the archive of a common history. Painful images of the past resurfaced, and I was forced to relive my many engagements with the police.

As a seventeen-year-old student, in a backstreet after school, an undercover police officer had pinned my body down on the ground, his knee driven deep into my back and his elbow repeatedly dug into the side of my head, grinding my face into the pavement. 'What did I do?' I pleaded. 'This is what you get for being a smartarse,' the officer laughed. The greater embarrassment would come a day later when I went to make a complaint at the officer's police station. Approaching the front desk with a cautious confidence at having the appropriate details, I provided the name of the officer who had assaulted me. Both officers at the desk turned towards each other, smirked, and while laughing one of them told me, 'Never heard of him'. Powerlessness set in. Standing in the middle of that police station, I felt tiny. Anger, frustration and weakness brewed inside me. Nothing could be done, and clearly nothing would.

Two years earlier, while I was on my way home from school, police officers had charged into the upper deck of the train I was on, past a carriage full of passengers and straight towards me. 'Train ticket,' they demanded. I had accidentally left my student ticket at home on that day, but no amount of reasoning or justification would deter them from issuing me a two hundred dollar fine. A fifteen-year-old, unemployed school student, I was forced to pay a fine I had no means of paying. A middle-aged white man in a suit turned to me after the police had left, chuckled and said, 'Sometimes it's just the luck of the draw, I don't have my ticket on me either'.

Encounters with police racism and brutality are not uncommon within my community. If it's not you on the receiving end, it's someone's brother, cousin, uncle or a local businessman being harassed by police. Indeed, recounting all police abuse would fill pages upon pages. But the majority of these cases are never brought to light. There is an implicit defeatism within my community, which is somewhat understandable. After so many racially driven encounters, we've learnt to play the position handed to us, to submit.

The police encounter is haunting. You sense the ominous aura cast over the street when a police van slowly drives past, scanning the area for potential 'suspects'. Everybody around instinctively shudders. Tensions rise. Hearts palpitate as people lower their heads under the weight of suspicion. Crimes we have never committed.

You see, we suffer from a chronic condition, all of us. A crime so grand, it is best viewed as a deadly disease or an eternal curse. A pre-emptive crime; one that convicts us before we even act. A crime so grave, it justifies having your shoulders dislocated, your head smashed against the curb or your face showered with pepper spray.

We are criminals, it's true. Guilty of Middle Eastern appearance.

Nicola Joseph has worked in the Australian media for almost forty years. During that time she has been a journalist, producer, presenter, executive producer and station manager at the ABC, SBS and in community radio. She is currently working on a PhD on Listening to Race in Australia at UNSW.

***Huna Amweero** is a screenwriter and radio producer. She has worked at Radio Skid Row, FBi and some unmentionable commercial stations. Huna is represented by Cameron's Management.*

'You Don't Look Lebanese'

That's what the nurse said as he wheeled me into the operating theatre. He continued, 'I'm Lebanese, do you speak Lebanese? I speak Lebanese'. I tried to not roll my eyes, and replied 'I don't speak Arabic, but where are your family from?' Funnily enough it turns out we are from neighbouring villages. 'Really?!' he said, 'I've never been so I wouldn't know. You really don't look Lebanese!'

The cognitive dissonance that Lebs in Australia experience when they meet me is simply because of the colour of my skin. I'm Lebanese, but I also happen to be Black – more specifically Namibian. I do my best to flex with Arabs, drop my family name and talk about my trips to Lebanon. But still I am met with disbelief.

Tired of explaining myself – I am deferring to my mother.

I am still waiting to encounter an Arab as decolonised and well versed in race and representation as Nicola Joseph. Interviewing her seemed like the best way to explain what it was like for me growing up. And how despite the racism and anti-blackness I still claim my Arabness with pride.

Huna: Are you ready?

Nicola: Sort of.

Huna: So Nicola, what was it like growing up Arab in Australia?

Nicola: I grew up through the 60s and 70s. My family came in two different patterns of migration. On Mum's side my great-grandfather came just before the First World War. He was an Orthodox priest. And then Mum and her parents and all her uncles and aunties came after the First World War. On Dad's side, his father, your great-grandfather, came as a sixteen-year-old boy. Arrived in Adelaide . . .

Huna: What year?

Nicola: 1897. The myth was that he walked from Adelaide to Toowoomba where he finally settled.

Huna: What?!

Nicola: I mean it's a myth. He kind of made his way across the country selling things, which is what most Lebanese did back then. Both families ended up in Redfern and by the time I was born everyone had moved out to the eastern suburbs of Sydney. So I had thirty-two first cousins on one side and thirteen on the other. That's almost fifty first cousins that were like brothers and sisters. The first ethnic gang in the eastern suburbs of Sydney.

Huna: So you had a strong sense of belonging?

Nicola: I can remember walking home from school and having people yell out 'wog' and spit and the racist stuff at school about my lunch or the colour of my skin. So I definitely felt like an outsider, but at the same time I belonged to this huge extended family and wider community. As teenagers we'd all go to these parties that were associated with the Orthodox community in Redfern. It was actually a really cool group of people. Some of them were great musicians and we had big record collections. We'd dance all night in the basements of big houses. It was such an eclectic group, A few of the guys (the good-looking ones) came out as gay years later and like I said, the music we were into was good jazz, disco, soul and RnB. But our parents would stand on the edges of these events with an eye to future marriages. There was a real sense of that.

And interestingly very few of us actually did end up marrying one another.

Huna: How did you escape the Lebanese version of *The Bachelor*?

Nicola: I started to feel suffocated by the situation. Every time I went out someone was watching you. I also didn't like the conservativeness of the family and that was a lot about patriarchy. I particularly resented the different treatment of boys and girls. I had also gone to a Catholic school and was sick of it. So, I planned my escape by going away to university. I discovered this really cool media course in Bathurst and I leapt from this protected life into the fire of being the only person of colour except for one Italian woman and an Asian guy. That was it on the entire campus in Bathurst.

Huna: Back when Italians were still people of colour . . .

Nicola: Yes. This actually predated SBS television. It was really interesting for me to be in this competitive media course where the lecturers didn't see a future for me. At that stage there were no female journalists of colour (I'm pretty sure there weren't any). Uni was also my first foray into living with white people, it was quite shocking . . .

Huna: What was shocking about it?

Nicola: Their attitude towards their families, the food they ate, just everything. It didn't seem to matter if they didn't go home for Christmas or ring up their parents. My parents were always turning up unannounced, which was really annoying, but they brought boxes of food. They were really shocked by how I was living, but also that boys were in the house.

I'd come home for holidays and there was always a ruckus. I remember one night I went out until two o'clock in the morning. My father found my contact book and was ringing up every friend asking, 'Where is my daughter?' My friends were a little scared of coming around to my house, and equally, I think my parents were terrified of my friends.

Huna: Why do you think they were so scared of white people?

Nicola: I don't think they were scared of white people. I think it was patriarchy. I think they were scared of losing control over their daughter. I was the first one to leave home out of all of those fifty first cousins. Mum used to talk about 'Nicola before Bathurst' and 'Nicola after Bathurst'. She saw a complete difference in me once I left home.

Huna: Taty means something specific, when she says 'Nicola after Bathurst' – what happened to you politically?

Nicola: When I left Bathurst, I went to Brisbane where I worked as a journalist amongst all white people.

But I did start to meet Aboriginal people in Brisbane. This was during the Joh Bjelke-Petersen era, where it was heavy apartheid. It was horrible. I remember, for example, going to visit Aunty Maureen Watson, you remember her?

Huna: Yeah, Granny Mook.

Nicola: Yep. I remember I was going to walk home from her place at night, and she wouldn't let me leave. She was worried the police would see me and think I was Aboriginal. I had a sort of certain political awareness, but I didn't have an awareness of what it was like to be Indigenous in this country.

Huna: Had you met any Indigenous people before?

Nicola: I did, in Redfern, but I didn't have any awareness about the history of what had happened to Indigenous people. When I came back down to Sydney, I got involved in the preparations for the protests against the Commonwealth Games and was part of a team of journalists who wanted to provide alternative coverage of the protests through the community radio network.

Huna: So what year was that?

Nicola: 1982. And this was when I really started to meet Aunty Maureen's family, her brothers and sisters and her children, her sons. One of them was Tiga Bayles who was a really good friend. I was running the 2SER newsroom at this stage . . . .

Huna: [surprised] *You* were running the newsroom at 2SER?

Nicola: Yeah, I had already worked in newsrooms in Brisbane and the newsroom at Triple J. Anyway, the manager of 2SER came and asked me if I would take on an Indigenous trainee. In walks this huge Aboriginal guy with a motorbike helmet, long hair AND I KNEW HIM! It was Tiga. At the same time the anti-apartheid movement was happening, and that movement had a group broadcasting on 2SER. Through the 80s there were also things like Rock Against Racism concerts that were collaborations between Blakfellas and some of the South African students that were coming to Australia after the Soweto Uprising. Everyone was really influenced by the black consciousness movement. Working together at 2SER, we started to talk with Aunty Maureen about how we could set up a radio station that was more accessible to Indigenous people so we took over Radio Skid Row and established Radio Redfern as part of that.

Huna: What was it like to be part of that?

Nicola: It was life changing in many ways. For me personally I can remember walking into the studios and people asking, 'Who are you? Where do you come from?' They were thinking I was Aboriginal because of my dark skin. I'd tell them I was Lebanese and they would ask, 'What's that war all about?' And I really didn't have answers. I was very much a Lebanese girl who hadn't been to Lebanon. I'd turned my back on all things Lebanese to distance myself from the conservative stuff around gender and family. Through Blackfellas prodding and saying, 'You can't come in here and think you're going to teach us anything when you don't even know who you are' I started to really take an interest in Arab history and politics. The Palestinian struggle and the war in Lebanon became central to my work as a journalist and later when I became an executive producer at the ABC and SBS I really took risks and pushed the envelope on Palestine especially. Radio Redfern led me on this journey really to think about who I was, not just culturally but politically. I was asking myself 'Where do I stand?' – not just in relation to the Arab politics but also to what's going on in this country in relation to Indigenous people and the Arab community here.

Huna: Is this when you realised you needed to go back to Lebanon?

Nicola: Definitely. I tried in '87. I went to Egypt with an Aboriginal woman, my best friend, your Aunty Kath who was Tiga's wife. We thought we'd get to Lebanon by boat through Cyprus because the airport in Beirut wasn't open. Then they blew up the ferry so they stopped that service and we gave up. Then you were born in '88 and that kind of changed things also because I had a partner who wasn't Lebanese.

Huna: Shall we digress and talk about that quickly?

Nicola: Yeah, I mean it was controversial me marrying an African. There's a real problem within Arab culture around the colour of your skin. You know my grandmother used to go to Lebanon every year for summer. And she'd bring back these little pots of 'bridal cream' from Syria, which was to bleach my skin. I think I was probably ten or twelve years old. It pissed me off.

Huna: So you grow up in a family where you got given bleaching cream because you were so dark and then you bring home a Black boyfriend . . .

Nicola: When I first told Mum and Dad that I had a Black boyfriend they kind of freaked. It wasn't a surprise to me, it really was just a result of the work I was doing and the world I was living in then. Eventually I got permission from my grandmother to marry him (which I was only doing to conform), and after that some Lebanese girls came out with their African husbands.

Huna: What?!

Nicola: There was another two Lebanese girls that had married African-Americans before me, but they'd sort of been disowned by their families. When my grandmother, who was the priest's wife, said it was okay for me to marry your father, the other families loosened up (sort of).

Huna: 1987, you nearly made it home. 1988 you had me. So why did it take ten more years to get to Lebanon?

Nicola: Well I split up with your dad. So I was a single mom. Which was another first for the family. I guess there was a feeling, and I think my mum more than anyone expressed it to me, she was worried about how people in Lebanon would respond to you as a Black child.

Huna: Jesus Christ! I didn't know that.

Nicola: How did that pan out though? Do you remember that first trip?

Huna: It was the best. I remember getting up every morning and running around the village to get my manoosh or my ice cream. I didn't feel unwelcome at all. I didn't even know that was an issue until you just said it.

Nicola: Yeah our family in Lebanon is pretty cool. Did you ever feel that way in the family in Australia at all?

Huna: There were obviously things that made us different. You were a single mom. The fact that we lived in the inner west and we were poorer. But it was different, my generation wasn't as big as yours and was more dispersed. I never really had big gang shit. But I grew up around so many Arabs and Black people, I never felt like I was weird.

Nicola: But you're not talking about the biological family here. You're talking about the other family I constructed around us. Tiga had nine daughters so you'd often be in bed with five or six other kids and getting up to all kinds of trouble. There was also a group of single mothers that came together to look after all our kids, so we could still build our careers. They were all women of colour and Black women. You also got to meet bell hooks when you were nine and Angela Davis when you were maybe about eleven because of my work in radio.

Huna: I'm seeing a pattern emerge about things that you realised were important to my identity. What was taking me to Lebanon about?

Nicola: For me it was about both of us putting our feet where our ancestors had been. That we got to sleep in the bedroom where my grandmother, your great-grandmother (who you're named after) was born.

I was really glad that even if there was kind of attitude towards you, it didn't touch you at all. I remember very clearly realising that the ancestors had recognised you because you were a really different child by the time we left. Something changed in you on that trip in Lebanon. And I just felt like they touched you in some way, they brushed you with the confidence of someone who knows who she is – you were glowing. What we should talk about really is that the only other Black people in that village at that time . . .

Huna: . . . were the Ethiopian servants.

Nicola: I was pretty horrified. I think that was just the beginning of that wave of Bangladeshi and Ethiopian women coming to Lebanon.

Huna: That's something I notice more now, going back as an adult – the slavery . . .

Nicola: I think in many ways it embodies all the stuff we're talking about . . . the racism . . . the colourism . . . and the gender and class issues.

Huna: It's the anti-blackness of Arab culture. Calling myself a Black Arab may seem like some 'trapped between two worlds mixed kid thinking'. But really I just want to defy the anti-blackness in the culture. It's important for me to talk about that.

Nicola: Blackness within Arab culture kind of depends where you're talking about. Because if you go to Egypt there's people that look like you who are African-Arabs. You go to Morocco same thing . . .

Huna: Well how does it all work then? At what point on the continent do you become African and at what point do you stop being Arab?

Nicola: I don't think there's any one simple answer to that. It's not as simple as saying there are people that look like you. Think about the enslavement of Africans we're seeing in Libya today. I'm sure if you asked Black Sudanese they could speak on the racism from Arab Sudanese. It's complex and mostly Arabs are not on the right side of justice in relation to Africans.

Huna: Totally, and just because I say I am a Black-Arab doesn't mean I deny Arabs are racist to Black people. But I still want to claim the space. To me that's the best description of the culture that I have been raised in.

Nicola: Absolutely. And so we've been talking about growing up Arab in Australia and what I find really interesting is that all we've talked about is how the Arabs see us and far less about how the mainstream sees us.

Huna: I'm finding that, as I get older, this doesn't matter to me. Looking at you and your work, I'm not sure it ever really mattered to you either. I see people of colour pursuing white validation to the detriment of their souls and often adding to the trauma of colonisation of Indigenous people in the process. How the mainstream sees Arabs doesn't mean anything to me because that mainstream picture still doesn't include me.

Nicola: It includes you in really superficial ways.

Huna: Totally, the whites have started in on African representation – and a lot of Arabs have their claws in that too. But when Arabs are calling for more representation, they aren't talking about me. I've called those Arabs out before and they only see me as Black. There is a fine line between being an ally and taking someone's place.

Nicola: Like that time that Arab woman kept writing about Black issues?

Huna: Exactly. That's why I'm much more interested community building and how that community views me. I care about my relationships with Indigenous people. I acknowledge my privilege, how the family did come here and prosper on their land. I try to be real about the benefits we've gained from this colonial experiment, from genocide. How do I even start to pay that back? That is more important to me.

Nicola: We talk a lot about white privilege, and I think in Australia especially, that term is too easy for Arabs and other people of colour – they're off the hook because they don't identify as being white. I prefer 'non-Indigenous privilege'.

Huna: That's something that I feel like we fought about for years – you didn't like it when I called you white.

Nicola: Ha, yeah. Well I did and I didn't. It was interesting because I would go to work and I was the darkest person there. But then at home I was the fairest person in the house and by then Jah Bya and I were together and you two didn't hold back, especially about the role of Arabs in slavery. I think I liked that, I learnt a lot about myself in having that fluidness and dealing with being challenged. All the ways that we try to categorise all of these things, you and I would agree, from the inside looking out, all of this sits in harmony. It's all me. It's all normal.

Huna: Yeah but I want to make sure that people don't think you're doing the whole Kim Kardashian and 'I don't see colour and that's why I can raise black kids'.

Nicola: Oh fuck no, I definitely see colour.

Huna: I guess what I'm trying to get at is, I am not fucked up as a Black Arab woman or whatever you want to call me.

Nicola: No, but everyone else is fucked up about you, Arabs especially.

Huna: I know who I am. I know my family history. I know where my ancestors are from. I know more about my Lebanese side than I do about my Namibian side.

Nicola: And that bothers you.

Huna: It bothers me.

Nicola: It bothers me too. Don't worry. It will soon come . . .

Nicola post script: I call on all my fellow Arabs to really think about this conversation in terms of their own work, whether it is in the media or the arts or academia. Too often I see us taking the place or substituting for people darker than ourselves. While the intention might be to be an ally, the result is often, as my critically thinking daughter points out here, the denial of an opportunity of those you sought to support.

A note from Nicola to Huna: Reading back on this I can see that you have got the tools to live in this country. I have many people to thank – it was not all me, although I know I did something right because you are so much smarter than me. The trips to Lebanon were important but I can see that circle won't be completed until you make it home to Namibia.

Farid Farid is a Cairo-based journalist and scholar. He has written for several Australian and international publications including The New Yorker, The New York Times, The Guardian, Vanity Fair, The Atlantic, *the* Sydney Morning Herald, SBS News, ABC News *and* The Australian. *His academic work has been published in journals such as* Social Semiotics *and* borderlands. *Follow him on Twitter @FaridYFarid.*

Holding the Line

Januaries are always the hardest. The sadness kicks in a couple of weeks after Christmas. I am referring to the default Orthodox one naturally. Summer melts away over a long flight back to Cairo from Queensland and my body is jolted back into winter's chill.

Teta's home, like most apartments in this cacophonous city, is poorly insulated, but I love the parquet flooring neatly arranged in patterns of four. It's where my mother grew up. I sleep in what used to be her room – not an attractive fact to mention when I am with other women, but it does come up sooner or later.

A few dates bookend January's significance: my mother's birthday; my cousins' birthdays; the 2011 revolution on 25 January that shook the world, taking down a tyrant in

Mubarak; and the celebration of the invasion that dispossessed Aboriginal and Torres Strait Islander peoples on 26 January, which somehow is still a vapid talking point for a perpetually immature nation still going strong in its unruly genocidal practices against black and brown bodies.

We arrived in Auckland on my mother's birthday twenty-three years ago, straight to Cho's Motel in Takapuna next to a Foodland, with twelve kilograms of schoolbooks strapped on our backs and an uncertain future ahead. Years later, once we had adjusted to being Kiwis and I had accidentally brushed up against the breasts of my crush on my last week in New Zealand, I moved to Brisbane. It was February, a month when things usually look up for me. I was there with my old man as he embarked on his first job as a qualified medical doctor in a western country. After a hiatus in the wilderness of migration where his experience treating patients in Egypt, Jordan and Saudi Arabia was summarily dismissed, we were on our way to middle-class greatness once again. He had worked in Bundaberg with Dr Jayant Patel, the Indian doctor mercilessly racialised as Dr Death on Australian news bulletins for months, and he also came into contact with Dr Muhamed Haneef, suspected of having a hand in plotting the 2005 terrorist bus bombings in London.

That first February with Dad, the apogee of our filial relationship, I spent hours lying on my bed listening to Usher's 'U Got It Bad' and wondering if my crush had read all the scribbled poetry I had written for her over many years, which I had hurriedly given her in a bag before I left for Australia. Weeks later in idyllic Redcliffe, north of Brisbane, I got into a solid virtual relationship (thank God for ICQ) with an Indian-Australian girl I never met. It had all the familiar trappings of an online liaison built on a steady diet of aching pangs of our budding sexualities, replete with moans and lurid nudes, and fizzled off a few weeks later in a deluge of tears and shame.

I missed being in NZ and having the Treaty of Waitangi, a public holiday recognising the sovereignty of the indigenous Maoris, fall on my birthday every year. I hadn't understood its moral significance or political weight until I got to Australia. There I was surprised at the blatant racism infiltrating everyday vernacular, especially in a state on which apartheid policies in South Africa were modelled.[1] Aotearoa, Land of the Long White Cloud, with its Neil Finn mildness and golden age of gangsta hiphop which I devoured, eventually receded from my memory as my sister and I adjusted our clipped accents – yet again.

This particular January – 9.15 pm on 25 January 2016 to be precise – I got a message from one of my closest friends. A week later I was moving to Berlin, to live with a German girl who would keep on breaking my heart and psyche. I had missed the revolution when it happened, but five years later Cairo had become a haunting, hollowed-out spectre of its former glorious self. Crippled and crushed by a brutal dictatorship. That eerie, rainy January night delivered a deathly blow.

---

1 M. Lake & H. Reynolds, *Drawing the Global Colour Line: White Men's Countries & the Question of Racial Equality*, Melbourne: Melbourne University Press, 2008.

Giulio, an Italian PhD student whom I'd met a couple of days earlier and was supposed to meet with that night, had gone missing. I dismissed my friend's palpable concerns as the paranoia that had enveloped our generation. Friends have been jailed, released and then jailed again; others have been killed and others are still missing. Our connections have become tenuous, threadbare. We are anxiously on edge when someone doesn't message back immediately, when phones are switched off; the fear of not knowing when we will see each other next. This has become our sinking reality that keeps on hurling us towards an unknown abyss of whose turn it is next.

I started to worry as the panicked updates rolled in. Mum was also in town, forbidding me from going out. I snuck out when she slept so I could allay my friend's fears as we searched for Giulio. 'Where is Giulio?' became our rallying cry on social media. A week later his badly bruised body was left a disfigured corpse in a ditch. Only the tip of his nose was recognisable to his mother in the morgue.

The first message when I landed in Berlin was Giulio was gone, murdered at the hands of an unwieldy police state feasting on dead bodies. The bloodiness and sinewy fleshiness of bare life was necropolitically unfolding before our eyes; these were bodies that we brushed up against and now their intimate corporeal impressions had left us. A graffiti mural in tribute to his short, brilliant, wondrous life uncannily close to my place in Berlin was a constant source of solace. *He died as if he was an Egyptian* was the tagline.

A few years earlier being Egyptian had inspired so much pride and promise. Young people, my friends at the forefront, had changed the stagnant stench of old men running our country for so long. The world was entranced by the magical realism of Tahrir Square. These tasteless platitudes are long gone but we are still out here. We are holding the line.

When we first migrated to New Zealand, Mum would sob constantly. I didn't understand that the pain of middle-class exile was a social phenomenon. The sobbing didn't stop even as we moved to Australia because the familial fantasy could never be intact. If only her sister was next to her; if only my grandfather hadn't died and been buried in Brisbane. All these hypotheticals turned to futile dreams of longing bore no fruit. Nothing seemed to work to fulfil 'the promise of happiness'. Diaspora was an unhappy, melancholic space and that was that. The infliction of violence in Australia didn't help either. Doomadgee, TJ Hickey, Ms Dhu lay miserably, deprived of all semblance of dignity next to Gika, Asmaa, Mina, connected in a global architecture of gruesomeness, an archipelago of terror, in coffins of sorrow. To break this fractured landscape, then you must leave – you must create your own 'alternative history of happiness' out of shared shards, remnants and memories of yesterday.[2] It is the only logical progression. You must be the Arab Pacific, in a nod to Paul Gilroy's *The Black Atlantic*, with its double

2 S. Ahmed, *The Promise of Happiness*, Durham, NC & London: Duke University Press, 2010, p. 17.

consciousness, inhabiting the twoness without searching for a wholesome oneness.[3]

So here I am in dystopian Egypt, in my own personal exile from family and friends in the arms of other family and friends, scrolling through timelines of outrage about Australia's brutality. I take it in then move on to deal with our own mounting losses. I miss Australia deeply on some days, especially when the blaring horns are on full blast or I can't navigate streets because of the broken sidewalks or when I see the dehumanising poverty Egyptians are experiencing – or when I'm drunk and I gorge on some of Pete Murray's elegiac songs. We wanted to change the small daily indignities of not being respected stabbing at your being and we did for a minute. For now we have to attend to the human calamities at hand. Ahmed Ziada has gone missing and finally showed up in a random court; Shady was supposed to be out but he's still in jail; and Alaa, who has about a month to go in a meaningless five-year sentence protesting against the no protest law, can't see his family, who have given us so much optimism and will, that it is too heartbreaking.

February holds the potential for the promise of happiness. It creaks open a new beginning, in Edward Said's sense of the term, ever so slightly with 'an unstraying obligation to practical reality and sympathetic imagination'.[4] Baladi

3 Paul P. Gilroy, *The Black Atlantic: Modernity and Double Consciousness*. London: Verso, 1995.

4 Edward E. Said, *Beginnings: Intention and Method*, New York: Basic Books Inc, 1975.

cafes are full to the brim with people watching Real Madrid or Al Ahly; patterns of smoke billow above us, and the public secret in our hearts – that a tyrant was brought down – remains tightly guarded. They can never take that away from us and that's what scares them the most. Political grenades from the daily pressures we are enduring are exploding in mute murmurs, just like in 2010. On every street corner those broken now burrowing in their torrential lives are burnishing with a sensuous fire for freedom and social justice. That this too shall pass.

In February I normally end up going to Port Said, from where so many Mediterranean migrants from eastern and southern Europe, as well as the wider Arab world, made the arduous journey to Australia by boat until the early seventies. It is now a hub for Egyptian as well as African asylum seekers desperate to be smuggled across the Mediterranean to Europe. Meanwhile other refugees from Darfur, Iraq, Iran and Myanmar end up in death centres, juridical purgatories devoid of humanity, on Nauru and Papua New Guinea.

The historic coastal town with its towering ports has its own chill vibe, away from the suffocating centrality of Cairo. Locals call it the 'corner of the world', where three continents touch. They consider it an independent republic as it resisted the invasion of the United States, United Kingdom and Israel's incursion after the Suez Canal crisis in 1956. Tragically, it is also where on 25 January 2012, a year after the 2011 revolution, seventy-four Egyptians were killed in a football stadium at the hands of military forces in a stampede on the pitch. This was and has been the ruling junta's middle finger to every anniversary. But in equal measure, players and fans alike commemorate their deaths on T-shirts and flags waved around ceaselessly. We take the blows and in this pugilistic death knell we punch on.

This February, we sat amid the rubble for one final jam session for El Toratheyah clapping and singing boisterously to folk songs of the traditional semsemia, a stringed instrument that traces its roots to the ancient Egyptians, as *jobat* or hash joints were liberally passed around. The authorities demolished the cultural centre dedicated to the folk art last week, along with dozens of other shops housed in the massive fish market slum area, to make way for a new mall. The politicidal will to destroy what makes us happy is all too palpable. A local police informant was there to watch on, unable to do much as we clapped and danced on around the fire in the blistering cold. For that moment, we held the line, we punched on, we were happy.

***Sarah Ayoub** is a journalist whose work has been published in* The Guardian, *the* Sydney Morning Herald, Elle, Marie-Claire, SBS Life *and more. She is the author of* Hate is Such a Strong Word *and* The Yearbook Committee. *She teaches journalism and writing at the University of Notre Dame, where she is a PhD candidate researching the representations of culturally diverse females in Australian YA literature.*

Pride, Prejudice and Pining

On Boxing Day just past, I attended a party held by a friend of my husband's at his home in Western Sydney. I had just checked on my children and rejoined a group, wine in hand, when one of the men began discussing the merits of his new hometown in country Australia. 'Ten minute commute, [something I didn't quite catch], no fucking Lebos . . .'

My husband glanced in my direction but didn't say anything. He just stood there, waiting for me to launch into my usual defensive. He'd heard it dozens of times before, his Australian-born Lebanese wife strenuously challenging the stereotypes that had marred her adolescence. But this time his wife looked around the group and noticed that no-one had questioned the racist remark.

And so I just stood there, silent, as the conversation moved on and the reality of what I had been fighting really hit me.

A couple of hours later, on the long drive home, I mulled over the man's words. My husband and children had fallen asleep, and I lamented that I was going into another year of my life still questioning my place in this land, the perceptions I had been fighting for a significant part of my life, the assumptions about my ethnicity and the conditions that came with them.

The next day I recounted the story to my sister.

'Are you surprised?' she asked me. 'Don't you remember that time in the Gold Coast, when that woman rear-ended Dad's car?'

'Those guys?' I asked, referring to a bunch of semi-intoxicated men who emerged from a bar in the aftermath of the collision, determined to help, only to get in the way with their back-handed compliments and racist observations.

She nodded.

'The one that looked at Dad and said, "Yeah sure, he's fine now, but tomorrow he'll be saying, 'My neck hurts' and the government will be paying him compo for the rest of his life."'

I winced.

'Yeah, I remember,' I told her. 'But I guess I also forgot.'

'Really?' she asked, tilting her head. 'I will never forget that night.'

I had always thought that racist experiences were singular moments in a person's life, one-off things that happened on a train or in a conversation and then afterwards you move on. But that afternoon, on that day after Christmas, something had shifted.

I realised that racist experiences were like little wounds that mark themselves on your person and stay there, like scars, reminding you of the storms you have weathered due to parts of yourself that you just can't control.

And that realisation led to a reconciliation of identity that had been a long time coming.

*

My first conscious memories of being Lebanese in Australia were ones of pride. My culture was something to be proud of. The alphabet and the colour purple had come from Lebanon, and so did Kahlil Gibran and Fairouz. Once upon a time people called Beirut the Paris of the Middle East, and even though war had ravaged the country, the Lebanese – wherever they were in the world – clung to that sentiment.

I always knew I was Australian, but I identified most as Lebanese. I saw Australianness in specific, sometimes stereotypical terms, and we didn't go to the beach and eat meat pies and have cousins named Shane. On Sunday mornings my parents would take us for Lebanese breakfast pizza after church, and we'd hungrily consume our *zaatar mana'eesh* and our *lahm bi agine* while we eyed my father disdainfully as he drank *ayran*. Sometimes we'd sit in the car for ages while my mum browsed the shelves at Abu Salim, which imported all the things you could want for a Lebanese pantry.

My experiences growing up in Sydney's south-west, attending a Lebanese Maronite Catholic school in Punchbowl and going to the village house every few months to hang out with dozens of cousins, were more Lebanese than anything. Even the diversity in our neighbourhoods – Shia, Sunni and Alawite Muslims, Orthodox, Maronite and Melkite Christians – resembled the land my parents left behind.

In St Charbel's, our Lebanese Maronite Catholic School named for Lebanon's first saint (a hermit, ironically, considering the fact that Lebanese people never leave anyone alone), we were insulated from the outside world. Surrounded by students who were like me protected me from racism and fostered in me a deep appreciation of my cultural and religious heritage. It gave my parents a peace of mind that is essential for most migrants as they navigate their lives in foreign lands. Nothing bad could happen to us there. They had found a home in the *ghurbi*, and now, decades later, stepping into St Charbel's still feels like going home.

*

I think we can all agree that adolescence is pretty tough. You're navigating bodily changes, questions about the future, changing friendships and a burgeoning sexuality (unless you're a Lebanese girl, in which case the sexuality kicks in promptly on your wedding night and not a moment sooner). When you're a migrant it's slightly worse, and when members of your community are newspaper fodder, you're basically done for.

I fell into the latter category, and the prejudice phase of my Australian-Lebanese existence began with the onset of the Arab-Australian moral panics on the cusp of the new millennium. The fact that I actually read the newspaper (dreaming that one day I would have my own journalistic career *Inshallah*) only amplified my growing awareness of my otherness, and I remember the years of year 10 work experience and first jobs as the pivotal moments of deflection and justification. When people recognised my Punchbowl accent and asked what my background was, there was always a 'but' after Lebanese. *I'm Lebanese* . . . *but* I don't know any bikies, *but* my father's not in gaol, *but* my brother's not a drug-dealing rapist who drives a $300K car while on Centrelink payments.

I should have spent my teen years sticking posters on my wall and obsessing over boy bands. Instead, I worried a lot about how the outside world would see me and constantly felt like I had to justify my Australianness. I'd made it through the two weeks of year 10 work experience, where I learned that Ashley could also be a boy's name and where white people could justify their racism by saying they had Arab friends – but how would I fare at university?

Not very well, I can admit now with the gift of hindsight. But back then I didn't understand why the Jewish guy kept his distance and why the girls were so fascinated by my nun-like life. They probably laughed behind my back, but I was so out of touch with the real world at that point that I didn't even notice.

But still, I tried to fit in without changing too much of myself. In those years I didn't hide the fact that I was

Lebanese, even when it would have been easier than facing people's ignorance. When I'd eat hot chips at lunch (having recently discovered the joy of chips with vinegar and tomato sauce) during Ramadan and people would question why I was eating, I'd tell them I was Christian. *Ohhh*, they'd respond, *I thought you were Lebanese.*

My lack of hijab probably baffled the crap out of them. And funnily enough, for some people it still does.

*

When I was nineteen I fell in love with a white boy. It was social suicide and I knew it. I was playing with fire and you bet I was going to get burned. My friends had warned me to be wary, my cousins had urged me to forget him, and in those early weeks of a courtship restricted to SMS messages (in case I ran into anyone from the village and ruined my marriage prospects FOREVER) I would wake from nightmares where my parents would disown me and I'd never see my siblings again.

In the beginning, the friends he doesn't see any more called me *Abdo*. I wasn't my own person – or even a girl – I was just an Arab to them. Beyond that, I didn't matter.

Who he was outside his ethnicity didn't matter to my loved ones either. My mother fainted when I told her, and I had to summon our GP to our home with the worst kind of symptom for an Arab parent: Disobedience by Daughter. My mother felt she had taken every measure to prevent this from happening – she'd instilled a sense of cultural pride and loyalty, sent me to a Lebanese school and banned me from watching the kinds of TV shows where people constantly slept with one another and girls lived out of home. She had stood her ground when schoolfriends came over and asked to watch *Home & Away*, and she'd discussed the merits of marriage between people whose parents knew each other in a way that wasn't at all subtle. And still her daughter had fallen for an *ajnabi* who was estranged from his father and had no God.

In between sobs, she fretted about what she'd tell my father. I alternated between moments of defiance (*What if he's my* naseeb*?* I'd wail) and determination (*I will break it off with him, Mum's right, interracial marriages do not work*) as the weight fell off my body and the smile disappeared from my face and I became a shell of the person I once was.

But I couldn't help it. I was torn between two impossible choices: my first tastes of the outside world, and my very curated (and arguably quite sanitised) upbringing which I cherished with every fibre of my being. Culture is so much more than ethnicity – it sits in the fabric of your daily life, on the plates on your table, in the art on your walls. It's the lens by which you see the world, the map of your existence, the rhythm in your body every time you hear a beat. And, I've since discovered, it's what determines your initial reactions when your children draw on the wall or put their dummy in the toilet. My Lebaneseness wasn't just a marker that described my biology, it literally made me who I was.

Throwing away the potential of a Lebanese partner was disposing of my culture. But maybe he really was my destiny, my *naseeb*. My cousin – a boy in the same grade at school – had told me that the Lebanese boys I grew up with would never want to date me while they were sowing their wild oats because I was 'marriage material' – the girl who was so obedient and traditional she'd still be there when they were ready to settle down. But this guy? He thought I had spark even though I was the plainest girl in the room. He wanted to have fun with me then, at nineteen, even if we couldn't go anywhere or do anything. Of course I was going to love him for it.

Some years later, after a trip to Lebanon, never-ending fights and countless pleas for the intercession of Saint Anthony of Padua (a Franciscan priest whose vow of poverty is even more ironic when you consider the number of Range Rovers and Gucci bags at the Lebanese Church on a Sunday), the white boy 'who never went away' visited my parents with his grandmother and mother in tow, as is our Lebanese custom, to ask for my hand in marriage. My mother accepted that his father wasn't there (but ensured we put his name on the wedding invitation lest the community question his paternity), and didn't seem to mind when his mother put milk in the (not-for-the-faint-hearted) Lebanese coffee.

I worried that I had caused my parents eternal disappointment, so I made it up to them by having the most Lebanese of Lebanese weddings, complete with folk dancers and traditional poetry that dumbfounded my in-laws and probably puzzled my guests. My husband's father came to the wedding, and we've been in touch ever since.

I actually thought my husband's whiteness would shield

me from the stereotypes and racist remarks, but still they kept coming. The prejudice was unwavering, and while no single incident was particularly damaging, as a collective they just reminded me of the conditions of my acceptance here.

Subconsciously I had internalised the racism and the bigotry. I didn't reject my cultural identity, but I toned it down. I was a model migrant, who assimilated and practised her cultural and religious identity in a socially acceptable way. I didn't commit any crimes. I didn't speak Arabic in public. I didn't play my Lebanese music too loudly in my car (if at all). I wasn't ostentatious, and if I wasn't ostentatious, I later realised, then I wasn't being Lebanese.

*

On the drive home after that Boxing Day lunch, so much went through my mind. In the days that followed, I thought more and more about my intersections, those tags of my identity that made it impossible for me to fit into any neat category. I'd never tick a single box and be done with it – I had been and would always be raced, gendered, classed and religious, and all the consequences of those various facets of my identity came out of those experiences coming of age in a Lebanese enclave in Sydney's south-west at the time of moral panics and gang rapes and the Cronulla Riots.

But I was tired of the shame. I had carried the prejudice about my community like a chip on my shoulder for so long that the pride became a distant memory. In its place was a yearning so strong. The prejudice had made me run, and in the process I became distant from the things that made me who I was. I had lost my language – words that once came to me so quickly and easily in a conversation now came out stilted and sometimes hilariously wrong. Lebanese music and dance had stopped being a part of my home life. I knew how to cook less than a handful of Lebanese dishes, even though I had grown up salivating over my mother's shoulder while she painstakingly rolled vine leaves and hollowed out zucchini marrows. I now had an Anglo surname and children who couldn't roll their Rs. Could I still call myself Lebanese?

A few days later I sat on my computer and started pinning photos of Lebanon to a Pinterest board marked 'My Ancestral Home'. I posted them on Instagram. I broached the idea of a trip back there with my husband. I wondered if I should start wearing my eyeliner the way that Arab girls did, because after years of thinking my white skin was kind of special, I wished I was more olive so I could at least look the part.

Suddenly it wasn't enough to just *be* Lebanese. I wanted to speak it, look it, live it. I was going to be a white racist's worst nightmare, not because I was particularly vindictive, but because being who I was – an Australian-born Lebanese girl – was my right. To embody my cultural identity wasn't discounting the gravity of the crimes that had led to those moral panics of my teen years, but it was resisting my need to shoulder the shame for the actions of the criminals because that's what the media expected me to do. Culture is not a prerequisite for crime, no matter how you frame it.

My parents had made the conscious decision to protect

their children from feeling that otherness too early in their lives. They had cocooned us in an environment where we could flourish, unaware of our difference, while growing up firmly entrenched in our cultural and religious traditions.

But cocoons have expiry dates and eventually mine came, and my flight out into the real world made me realise adulthood wasn't going to be as kind to me as my childhood was. I had sought validity and acceptance, I had criticised my people when it was due and I had pledged my loyalty to this country countless times, but where had it gotten me?

In that backyard circle, I was still, on the inside at least, a victim of racism. Even my white surname, my half-white children, and my white husband couldn't save me.

I was, in my heart of hearts, a Lebanese woman. I was a woman whose success had come on the back of her father's hard work and her mother's sacrifices. My childhood was built on long Good Friday prayers and *maamoul* at Easter, on stories about a fox attacking chickens and about the *natoor* guarding the garden. I acted on my compulsion to sing out a *zalghoota* at weddings – even my husband's sister's one – because without that *wililililililililililili*, it just didn't seem like a celebration.

And so prejudice gave way to pining. I pined for the Lebanon of Fairouz's iconic songs, for the customs that made my culture beautiful, for the richness of our dishes and the vibrancy of our weddings and the *jow* – the atmosphere – of our homes. I pined for a time when to be Lebanese was more personal than political.

And if I had to go through the prejudice to get here,

then it was worth it. Because in that circle of people in that Boxing Day conversation, the hate expressed by one man had been met with silence. But love – the love it gave me for my culture despite everything I had gone through – that speaks the kind of volumes that only an Arab *jow* can produce, with or without a *zalghoota*.

Carpal Tunnel

I faked aches and pains on that hospital bed.

I was six years old and the hernia operation had taken almost no toll on me.

Still I cried and moaned so that my mother wouldn't leave my side.

Little did I know she had no intention of doing so.

She held my hand and stroked my hair while I dreamed of all the *mjadra w fattoush* she'd cook for me as soon as we got home.

She knew all my favourite meals.

I must have etched them into her womb before she spent fourteen hours pushing me out of it.

The recipes are written in the curves and swirls of her fingerprints.

She worked with her hands.

God created them to knead *ma3moul*, chop parsley for *tabbouli* and roll *wara2 3inab*.

Just as much as they were made for twisting ears, pulling hair, wiping tears and forehanding faces.

Mama,

Hold still.

I will dig beneath every spot your feet have fallen until I have found the Paradise you stand on.

You've lost a daughter, and both parents,

Still you've never felt the weight of the world on your shoulders.

Instead, you crumpled beneath the weight of *our* worlds.

You carried the three children you had like a pack mule.

Never let us fall off, despite the many times we whipped you with ungratefulness.

Look at me, Mama.

Built like the brick walls you broke through.

Gifted with your husband's broad shoulders.

Climb on my back, Mama.

You needn't walk any more.

Baba.

We don't talk much.

Your silence that taught me to tame the West Bank within me.

You peel bills back whenever I tell you I don't need them.

You work with your hands.

God created them to fix faucets, battle naysayers and build gazebos.

Just as much as they were made for twisting ears, pulling hair, wiping tears and backhanding faces.

Baba,

Hold still.

I will knock on your chest till your heart opens,

And you let me into the Heaven you guard.

You lost two brothers in the worst ways,

Still the only weight you ever felt was your own, for you are made of stone.

You, immovable object.

Look at me, Baba.

I have your broad shoulders

And your booming voice.

Stay silent, Baba.

You needn't speak anymore.

This poem was written in two parts.
Before
And after
The carpal tunnel I suffered scribbling it down.
My mother held my hands and stroked my hair for three straight days in that hospital,
And she never complained of carpal tunnel
Once.

This is for the aching limbs.
The endless fights.
The sleepless nights.
This is for every silent treatment I ever treated you to.
I should never have treated you that way.
So I accept every forehand my face felt.
In fact now I think I'm grateful for them.
For the recipes in your palms must be printed on my jaw.

Whoever my wife may be,
She'll one day run her fingers down my cheek
And learn those recipes.
Maybe she'll cook them for our kids.
She can hold their hands,
And stroke their hair,
And one day
They'll write a poem,
Just like this.

***Abdulrahman Hammoud** is a Melbourne-based poet by way of Lebanon, blessed to have travelled the world to teach and perform. He's also founder of The Dirty Thirty Writing Challenge and editor/compiler of The Dirty Thirty Anthology. He's best known as an avid purveyor of starting books but never finishing them.*

***Asma Fahmi** is a digital news producer, mental health advocate and freelance writer. She is a founding member of several not for profit organisations and is a contributor at* SBS Life. *Asma has appeared on* Sunrise, The Project, BBC, The Living Room, SBS, ABC, Buzzfeed, *the* Sydney Morning Herald, 2GB *and* Al Jazeera English.

Millennial Dating

It was in London I saw it for the first time.

An ad with what could only be described as a picture of a cut of steak adorned with Cupid's wings.

Nothing wrong with that picture, right? Wrong.

It had the words *Halal meet* next to the picture.

Geddit? Halal *meet.*

Lord, have mercy. It was an advertisement for a halal dating site.

Other honourable mentions I encountered on the tube included a picture of a woman in hijab with the words *You had me at halal*, another with a take on Adele's classic 'Halal from the Other Side', and my particular favourite, a picture of Lionel Richie lying down next to the words: *Halal, is it me you're looking for?*

Ahhh welcome to the world of millennial dating.

You've got to applaud the snazzy marketing. As I looked at those pictures, I'll admit, I did snort loudly, but I soon noticed other passengers staring at the ad and then staring at me as if I was responsible for this madness. As a visible Arab Muslim woman, I felt a weird sort of guilt by association. I wanted to declare my innocence with a bullhorn, but I just sat there quietly and allowed people to secretly judge me with their eyes.

You're probably thinking the words Arab, Muslim and dating app are a weird combination. But you are way off the mark, my friend. Arab and Muslim dating sites are all the rage amongst, well . . . Arabs and Muslims.

Over the last few years many apps have emerged on the market. There was once shame about finding your partner online, now it's become the norm. You can swipe your husband or wife into existence. You can meet up for coffee and get that friend to call you with an 'emergency' if there's a code red (the prospective is a total dud). Or you can even cut to the chase and introduce your new crush to your parents, who will no doubt plan a big Arab wedding twenty minutes into the conversation. Many people have gotten married from these sites; conversely, many have sworn off relationships after using them. One user claimed to have seen his mum on one of the apps. Oh to be a fly on the wall during that awkward dinner conversation.

Before these apps became an option, the traditional dating scene in the Arab community in Sydney was less

Sex and the City and more Austen-era courtship. A hand-hold before marriage was, and still is, considered shocking in some circles. We also had a rite of passage to traverse; what we affectionately call a 'door knock appeal'. That is, a suitor and his or her parents would come to your home and check you out, and if both parties liked what they saw, they'd continue visiting until a marriage took place. Before you judge – it worked for my sister, who is now happily married to her finance manager husband and has two kids.

Growing up Arab in Sydney, I was subjected to over a million of these dastardly door knock appeals. The problem is, the Arab community is so small, often times I would awkwardly bump into one of these victims, ahem, I mean suitors at a Free Palestine Protest (let's face it, it's the only cause that unites the Arab world), or I'd encounter their mothers at a suitably woggy, low-budget wedding. Many of these suitors were walking clichés, a variation of Ned Kelly meets Muammar al-Gaddafi.

I rejected quite a few for a myriad of reasons and some said no to me because I:

- thought I was too cool, listening to alternative rock and being an emo before being an emo was a thing;
- would dress as shabby as the bird lady from *Mary Poppins*. My choice of fashion was a faux pas in the courting circles because you are meant to dress up to the nines and look your best. My theory was, if this is supposedly 'the one' then they should accept me warts and all. Oh to be young and so stupidly idealistic again.

Some of my encounters made for good dinner party conversations. There was once a time a strapping young lad wearing a very loud Hawaiian shirt came over with his parents. As I peeked through the blinds – like a stalker in a Hitchcock film – I saw him dragging his feet. He did not want to be there. Neither did I. So I did what was best: I refused to come out of my room and sulked like a bratty Arab version of Veruca Salt. When my dad beckoned me to come out, I yelled, '*This is child abuse!*' I was an adult. My dad chuckled and told the family I wasn't coming out. The next thing I heard was the door slamming as the family left in a huff. A-ha! Victory was mine! Now I look back and think, wow I was such an arsehole.

The vanishing act wasn't exclusive to this incident. There were dinner parties I refused to attend because they were just low-key marriage reconnaissance missions. I was arguing with suitors over such important matters as whether detox teas are a scam, why the Doggies are the best team ever and why pants are better than skirts. As you can imagine, the conversations were riveting. I was generally dodging the marriage ball left, right and centre – much to my mother's chagrin.

And who can ever forget the feeling of dread before coming out to meet the potential spouse? Venturing into my once familiar living room became akin to walking from death row to the chair. The first few minutes were awkward as hell as both parties were trying to scan the other without making it too obvious. Imagine having a guy plonked into your living room and you have to decide whether you want to wake up to his face every morning while both parents are looking on and dissecting every facial gesture. In my head I would always hear *Abort! Abort! Mission abort!*

I refused to serve Arabic coffee to the suitors and their families (coffee often signals the marching orders for the guest to exit stage left), as I thought it served as a cunning ploy to observe the prospective wife's physique as she did the Arab version of the bend and snap. Not for me.

The potential mother-in-law meeting the potential daughter-in-law is a delicate dance. The future mother-in-law keeps an eye out for a potential bunny boiler à la Glenn Close in *Fatal Attraction*. The future daughter-in-law assesses whether she has a monster-in-law on her hands à la Glenn Close as Cruella de Vil. They're both vigilantly looking for an inner sociopath.

Sometimes the prospective mother-in-law would come over to assess the potential like she was a track thoroughbred before a big race. One of my female friends told me she once had a suitor's mother look into her mouth to check if her teeth were genetically superior enough for her son. Understandable. Everyone knows the secret to a good marriage is strong dental hygiene.

But the pièce de résistance of my door knock career was Hairybootsgate.

A potential mother-in-law from an upper-class background – let's just say an Arab version of Lady Catherine De Bourgh – had come over to assess me for her son who was, wait for it . . . a doctor. You see, in the Arab Hierarchy of Marital Needs, the top of the pyramid would be doctor followed by lawyer, pharmacist and engineer.

I was dressed like I was going to the ski slopes in the ghetto. I was wearing an oversized camel jacket, my trackie dacks, a beanie and black hairy boots that looked like two Scottish terriers on my feet.

My mum took one look at me and was aghast. She demanded I change my clothes and try to look more 'feminine'. I changed my outfit to a soft lavender cardigan, a long blue skirt, and my hijab was prim and proper. I walked out and saw my mum smile at me, happy with my effort until she looked down and saw I still had my hairy boots on. I'd decided to tszuj up my outfit by keeping the Scottish terriers on. The look on my poor mother's face could only be described as constipated mortification. The next hour consisted of me being interrogated for my choice of footwear. 'Why did you wear those shoes?' 'Are you *that* cold?' 'Who *bought* them for you?'

The lady never got over my shoes. She never called back either. Heaven knows why.

And now let us set our sights on the Habib Bachelor Syndrome. It's kinda like the TV show *The Bachelor* except it's the PG version. There's always one guy in the community who attracts all the attention from the ladies because he has it all. All the girls flock to him because he's the kind of guy who can recite poetry, speaks French and Mandarin, is a medical doctor and plays the harp and pianoforte. He's masculine but woke at the same time. Every mother wants him for her daughter. He also looks like Brad Pitt circa 1995. This is the guy who thrives off attention, keeps every girl at arm's length, but in the end gets married to some hot supermodel astrophysicist within a month of meeting her and you never hear from him again. I hate that guy.

But all that has changed with the culturally and religiously appropriate dating apps – except for the Habib Bachelor Syndrome. He's now getting all the right swipes and is being stalked fanatically on social media. The popularity of the apps has extended to the 'real world' where apps are now hosting meet-ups for people to connect. That's the other thing: a lot of apps use generic terms like 'connect' and 'network' but everyone knows they're synonyms for engagement and marriage contract. Despite the wonderful tales regaled from survivors and victors of the door knock appeal, it seems more and more millennial Arabs are turning to the digital space for finding 'the one'.

Online dating lends for much more autonomy and allows users to avoid tricky situations like wearing Scottish terriers on your feet in front of Her Majesty, the Queen of Bankstown. It allows the user to put their best foot forward, literally. They can filter to their aesthetic tastes and use the right lighting and angles to project an image they want the world to see. Some say it's deceiving, others say it makes them feel good about themselves.

Marriage in the digital age is not just confined to dating apps. I've even heard of marriage WhatsApp groups, where family members meet and vet prospective suitors for their loved ones. If only Mark Zuckerberg knew he was also playing Cupid for Arabs.

These apps make a mint too. It's a profitable venture despite the varying success. One of the sites claims to have sparked over 100,000 marriages. Even if a fraction of that is true, it's not bad for a short amount of time cleverly curating a profile and choosing a flattering filter. And I'm sure many singles have lurked on the sites without actually signing up, just to enjoy the show. One profile earnestly declared he was 'looking for a Khadija in a world full of Kardashians'. Wow, sign me up, Kanye Khaled.

The traditional process never worked for me in Sydney. In large part I guess that's because I was a bit of an internet troll in the real world.

So I guess next time I'm sitting at home listening to Celine Dion's cover of 'All By Myself' for the umpteenth time, downing one halal aspartame drink after another, perhaps it'd be worth my while to click online, it might not be the only thing I click with.

__Wafa Kazal__'s home is in Sydney, but her heart is somewhere between Damascus and Tripoli. As a student of life and of the law, she knows the worth of words and hopes to always use her words in ways that honour their worth.

What's in a Name?

What's in a name? Likely more than my mother considered when she named me, and definitely more than most people think.

You see, the most visible Arab thing about me is, well, my name: Wafa (وفاء). Ultimately, it is those four letters that define so much of my experience of being an Arab growing up in Australia.

We Call Our *Baba* 'Dad'

He turned the corner and the sun was no longer in my eyes. I could see, clearly, how he handled the car – equal parts calm and collected, a leader if I ever saw one.

'You are in charge, Wafa. There is nothing to be scared of. You tell it to go, it will go. You tell it to stop, it will stop.' I wondered how often he felt that way. How many things were within his control?

Umo Frank looked over his right shoulder, asking me the question that both my siblings had just answered. I knew it was my turn to answer but tried to look distracted by what was happening outside the window. We had turned onto the esplanade now and were passing Brighton Beach, as we had many times, on our way to the city.

'So, what name do you want, Wafa?'

I saw the swing set I had been on a week ago. It had been a Mum weekend. We'd made an afternoon of coming to the beach, fish and chips and sandcastles included. I thought about the name she'd given me: Wafa.

'I like my name.'

'But don't you want something easier? Nobody knows the name "Wafa".'

He was right. I did want something easier. A name that required no spelling, no sounding-out.

We passed the long stretch of beach slowly. Women in hijab, talking and smiling. Children playing on the sand, swimming in the water. I thought about my *Tayta* and how much she loved the beach. How every time I saw the sand and the waves, I thought of her walking along the beach.

Wafa is my Tayta's name. I, her first grandchild, was named in her honour. In her light. When she introduced me, she did so proudly. 'This is Wafa Junior.'

I thought of all the names I could have, if not for my Arabness.

'Wafa is my name.'

Umo Frank faced the front again. He was not impressed with my answer. He looked at my dad, whose silence wasn't unusual. Umo Frank is his older brother. This means he has free rein to say what he wants, unquestioned.

Umo Frank was a stocky, simple man whose name wasn't actually Frank. It was *Fadi*. But he, like his siblings, has changed his name a year after arriving in Australia. *Abdul* had become Andrew and *Malik* had become Michael. Their children, my cousins, had been given Arabic names at birth but had since taken on new names. *Nasim* had become Nathan; *Yusuf*, Joey.

So, Umo Frank's question did not come as a shock. In fact, I'd asked myself the same question plenty of times – I'd fantasised about what it would be like to have a name that was equal parts pretty and discreet.

Being discreet about our Arabness was something my father modelled for us. He was 'Dad' in public and 'Baba' in private, and a different version of those people depending on where he was, when it was and who was there.

At eleven years old, I watched the man I knew so well (and, in many ways, not at all) mould himself to the people around him. Parts of me admired his ability to make himself palatable – something my *zaatar* lunches and school dress that sat past my knees did not often make me. Other parts were confused by his inability to remain true to either version of himself.

In many ways his dual identities informed my own. They let me shy away from Arabness when it seemed too much, too different. His changing between Baba and Dad gave me permission to change as I saw fit.

And so I did.

And so I do.

Mama's Warra Anab, Mum's Stuffed Vine Leaves

Mama's home – only ten kilometres from Dad's – was a parallel universe. Arabness was the fabric of who we were, what we did and why we did it. It was the food we ate and words we spoke.

Mama was 'Mama', at home or otherwise. Mama, really, didn't have a choice – she was visibly Muslim which, to most of Australia, meant visibly Arab. For her, and for us when we were with her, Arabness was not something we moved in and out of. It was who we were; whether or not it fit the mould of those around us was irrelevant.

With Mama, I learnt my resilience. I learnt that I would be found out, even if I tried to hide who I was.

'What is that?'

I had placed my schoolbag in front of me, hoping to hide what it was that Mama had packed for lunch.

Warra anab from yesterday's family gathering. *Tayta* and *Jedo* had come to visit, bringing with them fresh Lebanese bread for us to eat with them. Warra anab took hours to prepare and, if not for the bread slowing us down, mere minutes to eat. Fresh vine leaves stuffed with rice and lamb, best served with a squeeze of lemon, mint and radish.

'Stuffed vine leaves. It's an Arabic food.'

By the time I had mustered the courage to spit the words out, my friend was distracted by her own lunch. A sandwich. Nobody asks about sandwiches.

In time, I learnt to like the questions – these were the times that my Arabness, and all the difference that came with it, was interesting. I learnt to answer tactfully, carefully, slowly testing the boundaries of acceptance.

I still do answer tactfully. Making your difference digestible is easy when you've seen (and felt) the consequences of serving something less than.

How Do You Spell That?

To grow up Arab in Australia is to grow up knowing that parts of you are both misunderstood and unwanted by the world around you. It is to learn to hate those parts, to hide them.

It is to both loathe and love being told that 'you don't look Arab!' In those moments, you sit between the two versions of yourself, pleased with the moment of ambiguity but isolated from even your people. It is to, every day, ask yourself who *your people* are.

Ultimately, it is learning to moderate your authenticity. In doing so, it is internalising the belief that the world does not want you as you (truly) are. I watched my Baba make himself Dad. I watched and learnt that as even as Dad, he was not enough for them. The colour of his skin, and the sound of his voice – the things he could not control – gave him, and his Arabness, away.

If I have children, I hope that nobody asks them how to spell their name. This is not to say that I will not name them in line with their lineage – it is to say that I hope, for their sake, that their Australia is kinder than mine was.

While it would be easy for me to name my children John and Jane, it would do them, as it would have done me, a disservice: it would mean that they would not have to face their Arabness, and all of the richness that comes with it, every day.

*Born in Australia, and having lived all over Victoria and overseas, **Nokomi Achkar** now lives on Dja Dja Wurrung country. Proudly identifying as ethnically Lebanese/Greek and culturally Middle Eastern/North African, she is slowly making her way to visit the many places that backdrop her ancestor's stories, while attempting to unpack static notions of the Arab world. Nokomi makes art, writes, teaches, practises decolonisation, radical feminism and spirituality, and makes meaning through nature, women, ritual and food.*

There Always Was and There Always Will Be

In the retelling of stories, details are both embellished and lost, an art at which the women in my family are expert. Stories in our family always teetered around the edges of disbelief, embroidered with bright details but delivered with the nonchalance of the ordinary and everyday occurrence. Embellishments aside, what I know to be true is that there would be no story of me without the story of my ancestors, the women of my family; the matriarchs who taught me unshakeable faith in the capacity of the warrior woman – whether she is Ya Adra, Mother Earth or any other sage sister with a smile, a cup of coffee and wise words to offer.

Téta, my great-grandmother, taught me patience and gentle perseverance.

Yaya, my maternal grandmother, taught me stoicism and how to create miracles.

And my Mama taught me rhythm, love and to believe in magic.

Each taught me her art.

*

Our family came to Australia from Beirut. Before that Khartoum, before that Baghdad, and before that Alexandria. Born to this migrant family of wanderers who remained stubbornly and fearfully insular, my siblings and I are first generation Australians. Téta lived with us, and she and Mama pooled their resources to provide. Yaya was always close by (we called my maternal grandmother *Yaya* as a nod to her Greek father, but born in East Africa and raised in North Africa she was far more Middle Eastern than Greek). My maternal grandfather, the only adult male around, was frequently absent – figuratively and literally. Growing up we moved to a new house every couple of years and I'd joke that we moved instead of redecorating like some people did. In truth we were poor. There was no embellishing that fact. It became something of an unspoken challenge to see how quickly we could pack up a house. By the time we were in our teens – with enough cardboard boxes and tea supply *inshallah* – those women, and us kids, could pack up a house in a day.

Childhood was the scent of frying garlic and onions, the echo of music and multiple languages in one sentence, the chaos of moving boxes and being constantly, incessantly, inescapably together. Over the years my memories conflated myriad houses in as many different towns into a sort of timeline puzzle; I plotted significant childhood events by attaching the memory to the house we lived in at the time. In a world of eternal movement, it was an inner anchor of sorts. Walls, colours, gardens, street names changed, but our tribe endured with my Téta the lynchpin, the uncontested North Star, the calm in any storm.

Growing up, we lived so far away from metropolitan and multicultural Melbourne, where the 'ethnics' were carving out communities, supporting each other with belonging and solidarity. We were alone; four generations of Middle Eastern oddities with unpronounceable names; a single mother who wore hippie skirts; a family who spoke English with unrecognisable accents, eating a range of odd mixed-up foods, floating about in a perpetually steady, Anglo, working-class and bogan settlement at the foot of the mountains in the Yarra Valley.

Although I didn't have the language for it, I *felt* 'Other'. I didn't quite understand why the friends I brought home from school curled up their noses when Ma served *molokhia* soup for dinner, or why they didn't know the tabbouleh, haloumi or pita on the table and in our lunchboxes, or why they didn't burn *bakhour*, or why their Tétas didn't live with them. And yet I never felt Arab enough for other Middle Eastern families I met. We spoke French at home, due to the colonisation of Lebanon; the adults only broke into Arabic when they didn't want us to understand. As a white-passing person with an Australian accent who regretfully doesn't speak Arabic, I was often challenged to 'prove my ethnicity', constantly trying to prove my Arabness, to insert my credentials in order to belong somewhere.

And yet my whole life revolved around stories from Khartoum and Omdurman and Beirut and Baghdad. Our daily meals were *fuul* and *bamia* and *labanaya* and *kofta*. We sat around while the women used *halawa* to wax their legs, begging a bit of the sweet caramel toffee before it was all ruined with stubbly black hairs. We heard Yaya talk of driving her Morris Minor across the desert in Iraq, of swimming in the Nile and going to the cabaret in Beirut. There were the stories about sleeping on the porch in summer in Sudan and the time that they all awoke as a thief scaled the fence and bolted past them, only to be collared by Cousin Elias who shamed the thief for scaring the women and made him apologise. There was the story about when my Ma was six years old and they went to Greece for the summer, six-year-old Gisa came back speaking in Greek to her Arabic-speaking nanny, who turned to Yaya, bemused and confused, and said in Arabic, 'What is she saying? I can't understand her!' and Gisa sat on the loo puzzled that *she* could understand what was being said but couldn't make herself understood. There was the time they went to get ice cream and Gisa was so dedicated to her mango cone that as the car went around the roundabout and the door she was leaning on swung open, she determinedly held onto her ice cream in one hand and the door handle in the other as the car continued driving and her thighs dragged along on the bitumen.

With no Arabs outside my family to share my stories and sense of self with, I befriended Italians as the nearest cultural link. We had a similar sense of familial duty and our foods were sort of similar. They were also dark-haired and, well, basically weren't *white*! But it wasn't the perfect fit; their language, rituals, foods didn't make me sigh with the complete relief of coming home to myself. Only later, in the pages of Rabih Alameddine's *The Hakawati*, or in watching Nadine Labaki's *Caramel*, did I experience a sense of sameness and ability to identify with aspects of these characters' families, beliefs, customs and behaviours. In these fictional people I recognised myself and the legendary aspects of my ancestors.

*

Téta was made of the true stuff of an Arabian Nights heroine. Born Najla Abu Chakra to a large Maronite family in Haifa, she married a hard man who was by all accounts unyielding and demanding, a spendthrift in public but a miser in private.

While all the women in the family had stories about how mean he was, Téta had the patience and tenacity of Scheherazade herself: when Yaya was a young bride unable to boil rice, Téta taught her to cook; she taught my mother to sew with her trademark gentle encouragement; and somehow, a woman in Sudan with no independent income in the 1930s managed to save enough money to send her sons to school in Alexandria and, later, to always have a little treat for her children or grandchildren.

Téta had the self-control of a fakir. '*Oui chérie,*' she'd reply if offered something to eat or drink, '*un petit peu*'. Always a 'petit peu' or 'petit goût'. It wouldn't matter if it was a chocolate, a piece of bread or whisky, she'd always accept what was offered and never to excess. This measured behaviour was never more evident than in her cooking, especially her *wara aynab* or *kouroum mahshi*. Tiny, perfectly uniform parcels of grape or cabbage leaves filled with meat and rice and spices, packed into rows so tightly in the saucepan it was practically impossible to remove a single one without damaging the impeccable kaleidoscopic pattern and therefore making stealing one a feat held in the highest respect.

As a great-grandmother in her nineties, she'd beckon us individually into her room, the conspiratorial air thick around us. '*Vien chérie,*' she'd whisper, and we'd follow, knowing the prize for blind trust would be a date biscuit or bonbon she kept in a Walker's Shortbread tin under her bed. When Téta finally left Australia to live with her daughter for the last few years of her life, Mama occasionally employed a very white babysitter called Pam to look after us. Pam would arrive with that grandmotherly air, all matching lavender tracksuit, short permed hair, spectacles and – the never-ending source of disappointment for us – the same shortbread tin filled with . . . yarn. (Needless to say, we never *really* warmed to Pam.)

*

The first time I had sex the first person I told was my sister. The second person was my Yaya.

Magdalene Hélène Georgitsis was born in Ethiopia and raised in Sudan. She grew up fishing in the Nile and hunting in the desert with Bedouins. She was fifteen when her father died, and she was pulled out of school by a sibling who said she didn't need to study. Yaya wanted to be a teacher; she wanted to learn and had huge dreams for herself. In love with a man who was an inappropriate match, she married a man she didn't love because society and her family said she should. Then, heartbroken when her first child died at six months, she gave birth to *my* Mama twelve months later and sent the baby to Switzerland to be safe, never getting a chance to nurse her newborn.

When war in the Middle East made lighthearted living impossible, she insisted they get out and come somewhere safe. They had learned some English and when they went for their visa interview, she remembers the man at the Australian Embassy in Beirut telling them they were 'white enough' to come to Australia. My Yaya knew the art of making something out of nothing: newly arrived in Australia she made furniture out of packing boxes and crates. She practised her English (alongside her French, Arabic, Greek and Italian) to get a job as a social worker, helping all the Monas and Marikas and Laylas in the face of all those women who sniggered at her accent and pretended they couldn't understand her and called her Made*line.*

She smoked like a lumberjack and wore her long oval nails lacquered in Revlon Red. With a slick thick black bun at the crown of her head, she said flat English syllables with her unmistakable unplaceable accent and they morphed into musical sounds like ve-GE-tab-les and Ad-e-LAY-EED. And with that marked voice she pronounced irrefutable proverbs like: my *grandchildren are* twice *my children.* Naturally she was the perfect choice to divulge my late-night tryst to.

So on that Sunday morning, which happened to be my mother's and brother's birthdays, in between the *lahme* and the cake, I brought Yaya into my room, nervous and clammy, and told her my secret: that I had had sex with the boy I was utterly in love with, and that clearly I was now pregnant. She was immensely, unfathomably cool. She asked what time we'd had sex – making her cooler than anyone else's grandmother ever before or since, given she knew the magical secrets of the time-sensitive nature of the pill – and we hatched a plan. Monday morning, I got dressed in my school uniform as usual and went to the bus stop. Moments later Yaya arrived in her car, and instead of catching the bus to school she took me to the doctor. I got the pill and then spent the day at her house in her nightgown, snoozing on the couch, watching Oprah, playing *quartorze*, eating olives and *khobz* and drinking hot Milo. As it neared 3 pm I put on my school uniform again and she drove me back to the bus stop to walk the couple of hundred metres home and enter the house with Mama none the wiser. I was fifteen years old and Yaya never said a word to anyone.

*

Mama raised three kids with help from Téta and Yaya. In order to supplement what little she had, at various times she worked as a cleaner, a bookkeeper and a massage therapist, and performed and taught bellydance. Nearly all my memories of family gatherings include Mama performing for us in her turquoise costume. There were few times in my life I felt as special as when she'd glide around the circle of adoring admirers to George Abdo's '*Meenie Yaba*' and tease us with her scarf; my fingers crossed ferociously in my lap, I'd pray I'd eventually be the chosen one and she would drape the whole scarf over me.

When I first decided I was an artist – never doing *anything* by halves – I envisioned creating a giant mural in my bedroom, without any idea if I even *could* paint. Although I was hypersensitive to the fact that we had little money and worried that we wouldn't get our bond back, Ma said, 'It's okay, we'll wash it and repaint if we have to' and let me loose on the walls of our rental. I created a fairyland of magical toadstools and trees and vines, headed with the maxim, *Your talent is God's gift to you, what you do with it is your gift back.* As an adult I watch her with my nieces and see the same encouragement of creativity and play that she gave me all those years ago. Increasingly, parenting and educational theory extols the virtues of less structured learning and playing. Every time I read a new study on the benefits of playtime, I think of my Ma whose intuition led her to exceptionally creative and innovative parenting despite the fact that her own parenting had not been nearly as generous.

*

In my own journey and discovery of my identity and belonging, I asked more questions from the women in my family, trying to figure out what *they* wanted from their lives; what did *they* dream? Where did *they* fit? I have spent a lifetime trying to make sense of Australia and find my place in it. And as I've investigated and interrogated the stories of the women on whose shoulders I stand, I realise that my ancestors taught me indefatigable faith in women, ritual and spirituality.

The origins of some of our rituals cannot be justifiably explained; they have to be accepted with a pinch – sometimes a handful – of salt and a smile. While Téta was alive she would make the thick, sweet, black coffee in a long-handled azure pot with a spout. Too young to drink it, I'd still hang around the kitchen for the ceremonial-like event and to listen to whatever stories were being told. There was no question of whether one wanted their coffee sweetened or not, her ritual was a heaped spoon of coffee for each cup and one for the pot, plus one heaped teaspoon of sugar per person. Stir two or three times, always clockwise. Bring to the boil. Lift off the stove until the *boun* (the tasty dark foam) settles. Return to heat. Repeat process twice. Serve in small cups decorated with geometric patterns. Ensure each cup gets some of the *boun.* When she finished drinking, each woman would carefully place the saucer upside down on top of the cup, swirl three times clockwise and flip her cup over. You had to swirl clockwise so the cup reader could see into the future; if you swirled anticlockwise they would read your past – and set down the cup for the fortune to emerge and the *boun* to set. The 'fortunes' are variations of the same heartfelt hopes for each other: *I see a handsome man* (if you're single); *you'll have a child* (if you're newly married); *there's money here, see the gold coins* (if you're near retirement), and inevitably the final pronouncement, *maktoub* – look, it is written.

As an adult I make coffee with my mother and my Yaya, now eighty-nine. We sit, swirl, tell stories, share our hearts and read our cups. Regardless of how others may choose to label me, I know I am a descendent of at least three generations of courageous and loving and spirited women whose lives took them across the Arab world and eventually to a new life and new rituals in Australia. Women whose hands I see guiding mine, whose voices I hear echoed in my own as I answer my niece when she watched me make coffee and asked about the thrice-performed routine. I told her I didn't know why I did it, it was something Téta always did. Then I told her the story my Mama told me:

A young woman watched as her mother prepared the family's Sunday lunch. She saw her mother cut a slice of meat off the bone before putting it in the oven and asked, 'Why do you do that?' Her mother answered, 'I don't know, daughter, it is something my mother always did'. The young woman went to her grandmother and asked, 'Grandmother, why do you cut a slice of meat off the animal before you cook it?' The grandmother replied, 'I don't know, it is something my mother always did'. Finally, the young woman went to her great-grandmother and asked, 'Great-grandmother, why do you always cut a slice of meat off the animal before cooking it?' Her great-grandmother chuckled and said, 'Because, my child, my oven is too small!'

Sara Saleh

A Hyphenated Death

'The achievements of exile are permanently undermined by the loss of something left behind forever.'

– Edward Said

For a thing I am supposed to fear, I think of death often. Death and the logistics of being dead.

I can fit most things into a colour-coordinated excel spreadsheet. Death is no exception.

I can tick a box next to ablution (no decoration), prayers (no hymns), a cocoon of white cotton cloth (no caskets). Religion and ritual fill in the blanks. But one uncertainty remains . . . burial plot, To Be Determined.

How do I, mixed migrant heritage, daughter of accidental

geography, decide where my burial plot will be? Do I choose the anxiety of Jerusalem, my occupied ancestors and our occupied cemeteries? Should I consider my maternal family, exhaling the hurt and heart of Beirut every single day? Is Cairo, mix of chaos and my paternal lineage, a choice already made for me? Or . . . do I stay here in Australia, a country that doesn't want me?

For white settler communities, for those who have never been dispossessed and displaced in one way or another, this is a relatively simple matter.

What of fractured homes, and fractured identities?

*

As 31 December 1999 loudly slipped into 1 January 2000, as people partied through the arrival of the new millennium and breathed a collective sigh of relief about the Y2K bug, I was awakened by the startling noise of someone wailing.

Disorientation quickly dissolved into fear. I jumped out of my bed and ran outside into the living room. My father, unruly hair and chequered PJs, was consoling my sobbing mother strewn on the couch. I had never seen her cry like that before. I stood there, waiting, confused, tense.

'We just got a call from your uncle. Jiddo is with God now,' Baba said. 'Don't worry, *habibi*. Just go back to sleep.'

My first conversation about death. Just like that. And still confused, I went back to sleep. Just like that.

Mama was on a flight to Beirut the next day, and we continued, Business As Usual. Perhaps Baba wanted to protect my childhood 'innocence'. Perhaps this was a coping mechanism for adults. It was easier not to try and explain death.

I thought about Jiddo Jameel in the following days. His postcard sea blue eyes and stark white hair. He looked like a slimmer version of Santa Claus. He would always sing made-up versions of Fairouz's Arabic lullabies to me, and I (not my mum) had inherited his singing voice. I thought about his infamous, insatiable sweet tooth (also something I inherited), the way he always had a chocolate bar or a Cornetto drumstick in hand ready to be finished off. And how the last time I ever saw Jiddo, he chased me around the house with a stick, until three of my aunts could stop him, in a fit of diabetic rage that turned a beloved old Santa Claus into a broken man, withering away, in the eyes of his distraught eleven-year-old granddaughter.

I understood what death meant, kind of. Enough to know it was more than the fairy tales our parents told us ('we go to the sky as a star'), or what we saw in the movies (Mufasa still haunts us all). I knew I was never going to see Jiddo again, but I wasn't quite sure how to process his passing. And twelve was not the year that made me.

Even as adult conversations around me were happening. Even as my parents travelled to our home countries again and again each year to visit their parents' graves, as is custom. I continued to avoid death. Our Arab-Islamic paraphernalia around it. Its meaning.

It was easier to accept Western notions of mortality and clichéd euphemisms: 'you only have one life'. I did not want to commit to any belief of what happens in the 'afterwards'.

I was here and death was there.

*

Death found its way back to me at twenty-seven.

Atta, my paternal grandmother, my favourite person in the whole world, passed away after years of illness. It seemed sufficient then to write poems or post my old baby pictures with her captioned with what was probably a misunderstood Rumi line.

Mourning seemed like theatre, and I was too tired, too sad to speak, to respond to a shedding of '*Allah yerhamas*' and 'my condolences' that followed us from the mosque *janaza* prayer and Quran recitation gathering, to the *dua* circles held at our house every single night for a week.

I was expected to be a universal version of dignified and graceful even in grief – to make myself accessible whenever loved ones and strangers and acquaintances demanded it.

I have spent most of my life navigating white spaces, moulding myself and managing the centering of whiteness – that even when there's a possibility of bringing more of myself into a room, my whole grieving self, I don't know how.

So I remained quiet for most of 2014, and there are many ways to be quiet. Told everyone I was fine. Worked it away. Performed it away. Prayed it away. This is how we carry ourselves – death in Diaspora. You learn to keep surviving even when pieces of you do not.

I was grateful to a handful of my aunties and uncles, stacks of cousins (not by blood but bonded in our attempts to find familiar in foreign lands, to find homes in people) and friends. They came during the quiet of the day, checking in, bringing pastas and salatas, which we barely touched, asking what else we needed.

We don't talk about grief, but we don't talk about it together. In our exile, our anxieties are shared. We look after each other. I sat with myself, suspended in scripture, or surrounded by my immediate community – there were no performances. No self-corrections. I didn't have to filter my feelings, even in my quiet . . . I could disassemble these scraps of armour.

In Diaspora, we find different ways to carry old and new griefs. We carry it with each other, for each other.

*

Almost a year later I was supposed to be meeting a colleague at Paper Cup, a café on Sydney's Cavendish Street. It happened to be right across from my old primary school in Stanmore. I hadn't been there in years – the return triggered a holy well of nostalgia.

While my parents were working multiple jobs during the day and studying endless nights between them, my bonneted Atta, like an Arab Jane Austen, would walk me up and down Cavendish for school drop-off and pick-up.

Each day started with an awkward nod as she signed me in at 8.45 am and ended with a 'sank-yew' at 3 pm. Atta barely spoke a word of English, but everyone knew who she was. I made sure of it. 'My Atta made me *malfoof* . . . My Atta braided my hair today . . . Atta taught me to play this card game called Donkey,' I would tell my teachers, my classmates, anyone who would listen.

I walked past the cafe (presumably my colleague was waiting for me inside) and continued up to the school playground. I peered through the iron gate. The monkey bars where my little body got its first bee sting were gone, replaced by some sort of contraption that seemed 'safer' (but what did I know).

Adjacent to the playground were benches where the sausage sizzles and bake sales used to be held. Where I cried and cried when my teacher Ms Sunny said I was a 'Muslim' – she was explaining why she had to refuse my request for a sausage roll even though all the other kids had one. Devastated, seven-year-old me explained to Ms Sunny, 'I am Australian, not Muslim.' Seven-year-old-me didn't want homeland on my body.

That afternoon, as I walked back to Paper Cup, I decided to go to Egypt.

Four countries, four flights and forty-eight hours later, I was in Hamidiya, my grandmother's village, a two-hour drive from Cairo.

'Welcome, *ya khawajaya*,' my uncle joked. Foreigner. 'We're glad you could finally make it.'

Atta was buried with her nuclear family members, most of whom I had never met. Atta's husband, my paternal grandfather, was buried with his own family in their village of Khers, another hour's drive away.

As I faced the tombstone, folding myself into prayer and reciting the words of '*al-Fatiha*' – '*Al-hamdullilah rab al-3alimeen. Ar-rahman, Ar-rahim*', I did not burst into tears as I'd worried I might. Instead, I panicked.

I was going to be so far away from Atta. Would I be buried with Jiddo? Mama and Baba? Where would my siblings be? What if I one day had kids of my own? I had always thought that as migrants, our tragedy was in the living. Our existence a constant hyphenation.

This was the first time I realised our death is hyphenated too.

*

Where will I be buried? In migrating, our parents had left parts of themselves behind. Our heirlooms were intergenerational loss and trauma. Survival was more than losing language or cultures whole. Survival was missing Rania giving birth, and Ahmed's wedding, and Hadi's car crash and his three terrifying months in hospital, and Teta's constant complaining—'This country is shit but I never want to leave it'—and *Khalo*'s cancer, and summer balcony nights until *fajr*, and my *Khalto*s fighting over whose turn it was to stay with Teta, and . . . Atta's death.

These missing parts aren't lost, they are atrophied. As if they are frozen in place, they never come with you.

Survival was also privilege. Was a blue passport. Was being anchored in three degrees. Survival was resentment, was 'I want to be normal, I hate being different'. It was speaking differently to our parents. It was: we are definitely speaking another language they can't understand. Passing through doors that were never unlocked for them. It was telling them we know better. Was 'Muslimah excellence'. Living as subjects in an overtly and subtly racialised regime. Survival is having an illusion of choice. Of old country and new. Of neither old country nor new.

Of which home? Of where?

*

Dad was asleep after the surgery, and wasn't expected to wake up for hours according to 'Betty', the chatty nurse who popped in every 15 minutes to check up on us. Her kind reassurances did nothing to stop Mama from pacing back and forth in the tiny room, steps synchronised to the beeping machine, face scrunched up like a paper bag.

I suggested we go get a coffee (decaf for Mama), but Mama was reluctant to leave. Nurse Betty seconded the notion. I took Mama's leathery, cold hand and led her outside. We sat together in the hospital's central lobby, which was bookmarked by an over-priced flower shop, bright floral arrangements and pink teddy bears spilling out of it, and a cafeteria with a very long line of people waiting for crappy hospital coffee.

'Mama, who do you want to be buried with? Are you going to pick me, your favourite child, to hang out with in the afterlife? Or Teta, who has like eight other children she can choose from? Think about it carefully.' I wriggled my eyebrows.

'I think we should talk about it soon,' she said.

'Mama, please.' I squeezed her knee.

'Sara . . .' Mama's voice strained. 'As migrants, death is

much like our notion of *watan*. It expands and shrinks. Progresses and regresses. It does not wait for permission or invitation. Death just is. And it is inevitable. We are born in one place and buried in another. In exile, we live and die several times over in between. How blessed are we that this spans continents and countries and cultures.

'Your life is not defined by where you are buried, or by words on a tombstone, but by story, and memory – this is what we inherit, this is an exile's legacy, *watan* never leaves you. In death, we demand a respect that we don't always get in life. That is what our dying looks like.'

We never did talk about dad's surgery that day, his diagnosis, or the worst-case that it might bring, despite the spectres of "what-if" and grief that follow us around. But Mama's words finally alleviated my other-worldly worries, they balmed past wounds I had not visited for a long time. I thought of Atta, that I was her legacy, and realised then that I did not need to find my place in death. I always had a place in the people I love, the ones I call my *watan*. I just hope I am theirs.

Randa Abdel-Fattah

Seventy-One Years of Words

Every year, every commemoration of the Nakba of 1948, we Palestinians are expected to write and to speak. It's been seventy-one years of words now. Hundreds of thousands of words of pain, trauma, hope, despair, rage. Words about laws violated; about definitions and principles that must be unpacked, deconstructed, laid bare with more words. Words of reason and restraint. Dispassionate, factual, clinical, analytical words that will persuade the world that there is a human being behind the ink.

There are other words too. Words in blood; words that stretch beyond the page and screen and pierce the heart. Words that demand we are heard, that seek to press deep into the flesh and heart of our audience.

Seventy-one years of words.

Poets, lawyers, activists, bloggers, teachers, academics, journalists.

Testimonies and commentary, human rights reports and legal analysis: refugees, water, illegal settlements, peace process, arms deals, Ahed Tamimi, checkpoints, UN resolutions, status of Jerusalem, the Great March of Return, apartheid state, Boycott, Divestment Sanctions.

Here are the words in the historical archives: ethnic cleansing and right of return.

Here are the laws and resolutions: illegal occupation, illegal settlements, crimes against humanity.

Here are the statistics, the live tweets, the word 'PRESS' written on the vest, the grotesque spectacle of a Eurovision contest.

Each year I am expected to write about why the struggle for our freedom is a just one. To present 'my side' of the conflict. Because White guilt only wants op-eds.

If people want to know what is happening, if they care, the words are all there. So be with us, or be against us – openly, or in one's 'neutrality'. Choose the words to heed and the words to ignore.

After seventy-one years, I'm done trying to persuade people of our cause. It needs no defence, no humanisation, no legitimising. My words are no longer an argument. We won the argument at Deir Yassin, in the UNRWA refugee camps, in the buried villages, the stateless generations, the live bullets at protestors in Gaza, the billions of Western dollars cashing up what the UN, South African diplomats and former anti-apartheid activists – including Jews – have described as an apartheid state.

Each year I want to simply bear witness about what being a Palestinian in the diaspora means for me.

Dispossessed. Settler

I am writing this on the land of the Darug people. I was born in Sydney in the year the National Aboriginal Conference called for a treaty between Aboriginal people and the Australian government. A treaty that has, forty years on, still not been achieved. I am here only because my father earned a scholarship to Sydney University in 1972, a time when the last vestiges of the White Australia policy were being dismantled. My father was a stateless Palestinian because the same imperial government that colonised and stole Australia set the course for the colonisation and theft of my father's homeland, Palestine. I am writing this essay on the land of the Darug people and not in, say, Cairo, my mother's birthplace, because my mother migrated to Australia in 1974. Her family saw no future in Egypt following Gamal Abdel Nasser's nationalisation of Egypt's economy in the 1970s. My mother's family left a country in the throes of resisting years of British colonialism and imperialism only to migrate to a former British colony because its government decided their brown skin was now palatable. I am the child of the dispossessed. And I am complicit in dispossession. I know that this country's wealth is bloodstained and that the ships that invaded these shores more than two hundred years ago were built and financed by Britain's slave trade. We are endlessly reminded of our proud British heritage, of our inherited values and institutions. The bloodstains are almost always covered up.

I know that I live on bloodstained land.

Who do you think you are?

I turn on the television and I watch *Who Do You Think You Are?*. I watch people's histories traced through documents and archives, museums and civil registries. I see the privilege of continuity, of unbroken chains of biography and family. Research: the luxury of colonisers.

Will somebody tell me what happened to my father's great uncle in Jaffa in the early 1930s? All the family knows is that he was hanged during the Arab Revolt. Was he one of the men executed by the British? Where is he buried? Did he have a diary? What exactly was his role in the uprising against the British? What would he say if he knew Palestinians were still demanding independence?

Who do you think you are? I know who I am and who took away my ability to know my ancestors.

Burqa

The house is grey limestone with an arched green front door. It's nestled on a huge block of olive trees. The limestone retaining wall is slowly crumbling, parts of it have gone missing. An empty, unprotected house, blocks of stone are missing, stolen by people in the village.

Burqa, a village in the West Bank. A population of just

about 2600 people in 1945, the year my father was born. Three years before the Nakba, before their lives and destinies would be shattered.

Burqa is perched high up in the mountains, surrounded by a horizon of blue sky and stretches of mountains and hills. A modest, unpretentious and resilient existence, Burqa survives. The year I visit, I notice the watchful sentinel eyes of an illegal Jewish settlement that stands at the top of a nearby mountain. I feel rage.

During our bus ride on our first trip to his village, my father sits upright in his chair, hands fidgeting, legs shaking, eyes drinking in a landscape long missed. As we climb a slope our bus driver stops on the side of the road to let out two of the passengers, a father and son.

After both disembark, the elderly man pops his head through my father's window and asks: 'How much do you remember?' My father looks him directly in the eye. 'Everything.'

We continue on, and as we pass a dilapidated hut where a small group of children sit upon the remains of a fallen fence, my father suddenly cries out: 'That hut! It was a police station. Right?' The bus driver nods.

Suddenly the dusty, narrow road opens into a fork and my father draws in a sharp breath as the houses tower around us. 'Burqa,' his choked voice whispers.

'My primary school!' my father shouts as we pass a small blue building. Our bus driver sounds the horn and some children playing in front turn to look at us, waving at us as we drive on. We turn down a gravel road and my father grins as he points out the mosque he had prayed in with his father as a child.

Mosque
In 2011 Jewish settlers deface and then set fire to the mosque.

Grave
The year 2000. My father can't find his father's grave. Shrubs and weeds blanket the graveyard. Silently and solemnly he hops from one spot to the other, careful where to place his feet. He pauses, frowns as he inspects the piece of paper in his hand. Instructions on where he might find it, given to him by his mother, from the family's cramped apartment in Jordan where they are all forced to live.

He becomes more frantic, rubs dirt off gravestones, tries to decipher faded words on stone. Eventually he gives up and returns to the car. We drive on in silence.

The Zionist project in Palestine severs families: both the living from the living, and the living from the dead.

Goodbye
Eleven years later, on our second and last visit, we find my grandfather's grave. We say goodbye. Who knows if the Israelis will allow us to return?

Political
I speak at a rally protesting our government's red-carpet welcome to Benjamin Netanyahu. A few weeks later, a North Shore girls' private school cancels my keynote speech.

They are very accepting of diversity and so on, but I am too political.

I am too political.

Balance

'Could you please insert a balancing sentence condemning Hamas rocket fire?' an op-ed editor asks me. 'The Opinion page is not a place for tit for tat,' is what a senior editor of one of Australia's leading newspapers tells me when I seek a right of reply to an article published by a spokesperson of the Australia/Israel and Jewish Affairs Council.

'Do you have any contact with people in Gaza who have been affected by the bombs but who are also opposed to Hamas firing rockets into Israel?' a reporter enquires.

'We would like to get both sides of the argument here today. We'll start with you first, Randa. Could we get your side of the story and then we'll get the other side . . .?' Oh, but this is a conflict of equal sides, of relative truth, of a middle road if only the parties took steps to reach it. If only they'd talk to each other!

Balance: I have an image of a seesaw. The illusion of a balancing structure is there, but what counts is the weight distribution.

Blockade

A Palestinian friend in Perth reaches out on Facebook: her mother is in the last stages of cancer, in unbearable pain, and her pain relief is no longer available in Gaza due to Israel's blockade. Does anybody know how her mother can access the tablets? Messages of support flood her page. She manages to make contact with somebody who knows somebody who smuggles in the medicine. Temporary pain relief until the tablets run out and another Facebook plea for help.

No need. The mother passes away a few weeks later.

They kill Palestinians with bullets, missiles and bombs. But they kill many more slowly, quietly, without a trace.

What is the hashtag for death by occupation?

Occupation

The brother of our oldest family friend, also my husband's relative, is in his seventies and has a heart condition. He also has an Israeli settler condition. Every week he defends his land against their encroachments and harassment. Every week an altercation, a battle; an old man against a young mob. Seven kilometres by foot, there and back. He dies in his sleep after another altercation.

Tell me again, what is the hashtag for death by occupation?

'Futurity'

I sit in an academic conference in Sydney early this year. I listen to an Indigenous woman, a Mvskoke scholar from the University of New Mexico, speak about Indigenous feminist scholarship and methodologies. As she speaks, I blink back tears; not of pain, but joy. The joy of words resonating, connecting. She talks about 'futurity', what she defines as '*carrying the unactivated possibilities of our ancestors who were cut down*'. Her words wrap around me like a warm blanket. I feel safe in these words. They offer me meaning, clarity. Why do I fight for Palestine? How does my fight now honour the people who came before me? Family members dispossessed, thrown out, dehumanised? What has always just felt instinctive and natural to me has suddenly been articulated. I am trying to activate the wishes, dreams and rights of my ancestors, of people like my great-uncle who were 'cut down'. I am trying to disrupt the trajectory of suffering and oppression by carrying on their struggle. I never knew my great-uncle or my grandfather, but in that moment I felt closer to them than I ever had before. I thanked the scholar at the end of her talk. And then I hugged her. For diaspora is confusing and messy. In giving me words to make sense of my place in it, she had gifted me my ancestors. Their purpose then, and my purpose now, binds us.

Witness

We start to speak, to write, and we do not know when or how to stop because it is unending. The Nakba is not an anniversary, it is repeated every day across the West Bank, Gaza, Israel, the refugee camps, in the diaspora. Seventy-one years of bearing witness. Seventy-one years of millions of testimonies. We write and we speak because it is all we have left.

Acknowledgements

Thank you Mathilda Imlah, Danielle Walker and Clare Keighery at Picador for being such a supportive and visionary publishing team. Thank you for sharing your expertise and your time with such generosity. Creating this anthology has been a joyful and cathartic experience thanks to you all.

Thank you to all those who took the time and effort to submit a piece to this anthology. *We are here, we are here, we are here.*

Thank you to the writers and poets in this book for having faith in our vision and for trusting us with your stories. We are honoured to bring and bind our voices together.

Randa and Sara

This is ultimately a book about storytelling and so I want to thank the greatest storyteller in my life, my mother's mother, 'Ana'. You taught me to pay attention to the details, to be curious about the moments in between, to delight in the theatre that is life. I don't know where I truly belong but one place I am completely at home is in your presence.

Randa

To Randa, thank you for the foundations and the friendship. You are an eternal teacher.

To my family, thank you for allowing me to be brave enough and stubborn enough to dream. For reminding me to tell our stories. We carry our history with each other, for each other.

To Atta, I keep you close.

Sara